Careers Theme Mate

The activities in this book provide teachers with a way to use the topic of careers as a creative and interesting theme unit that stretches across the curriculum. Students will practice skills in language arts, mathematics, science, social studies, art, and music. Many of the activities may be used in cooperative learning groups or by individual students. Although this book is designed as a whole language tool for teaching a unit on careers, the activities may also be used independently at any time during the school year.

Author: Peggy Hapke Lewis

Y0-EIK-985

COPYRIGHT ©1995 McDONALD PUBLISHING CO.

THEME MATE TITLES

Farm Animals   Dinosaurs
Weather   Transportation
Careers   Water
The Environment   Space
Patterns   The Five Senses
Plants   Wild Animals
Seasons   Pets
Communities   Things That Fly

McDonald Publishing Co.
567 Hanley Industrial Ct.
St. Louis, MO 63144-1901

Language Arts

Ask students what they think a job is. After they express their ideas, discuss the fact that a career is a job someone learns to do for a living and plans to do for a long time. Explain that your career is teaching. Allow students to say the names of other careers they know. Record the careers on the chalkboard. Next, see if students can think of categories some of the careers fit into (e.g., health care, education, manufacturing). Write the different categories as headings on large pieces of paper, and list appropriate careers under the headings. Allow students to add other careers to the lists as they think of them. Post these lists in the classroom for future use during the unit on careers.

Language Arts

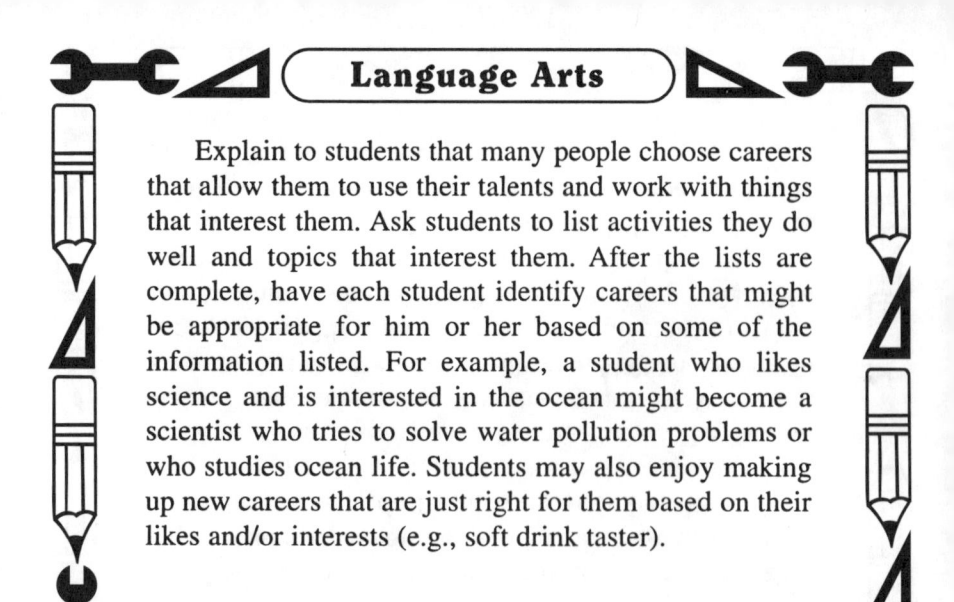

Explain to students that many people choose careers that allow them to use their talents and work with things that interest them. Ask students to list activities they do well and topics that interest them. After the lists are complete, have each student identify careers that might be appropriate for him or her based on some of the information listed. For example, a student who likes science and is interested in the ocean might become a scientist who tries to solve water pollution problems or who studies ocean life. Students may also enjoy making up new careers that are just right for them based on their likes and/or interests (e.g., soft drink taster).

Language Arts

Write the following saying on the chalkboard: *A picture is worth a thousand words.* Ask students if they know what the saying means. If not, explain that it means a person would have to use many words to describe everything one picture shows.

Tell students that a photographer is a person who makes a living by taking photographs. Provide students with a variety of magazines. Have each student find and cut out a picture. Ask younger students to create sentences that describe what the pictures show. Older students can write descriptive paragraphs about the pictures. Encourage students to use details when describing the objects, people, animals, colors, etc. shown in the pictures.

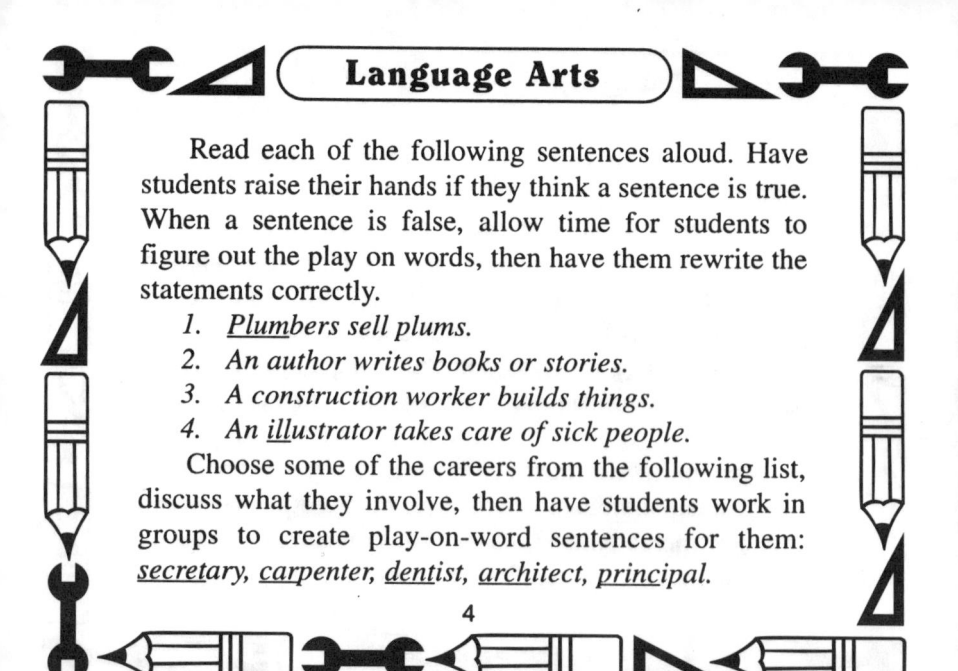

Language Arts

Read each of the following sentences aloud. Have students raise their hands if they think a sentence is true. When a sentence is false, allow time for students to figure out the play on words, then have them rewrite the statements correctly.

1. _Plumbers sell plums._
2. _An author writes books or stories._
3. _A construction worker builds things._
4. _An illustrator takes care of sick people._

Choose some of the careers from the following list, discuss what they involve, then have students work in groups to create play-on-word sentences for them: _secretary, carpenter, dentist, architect, principal._

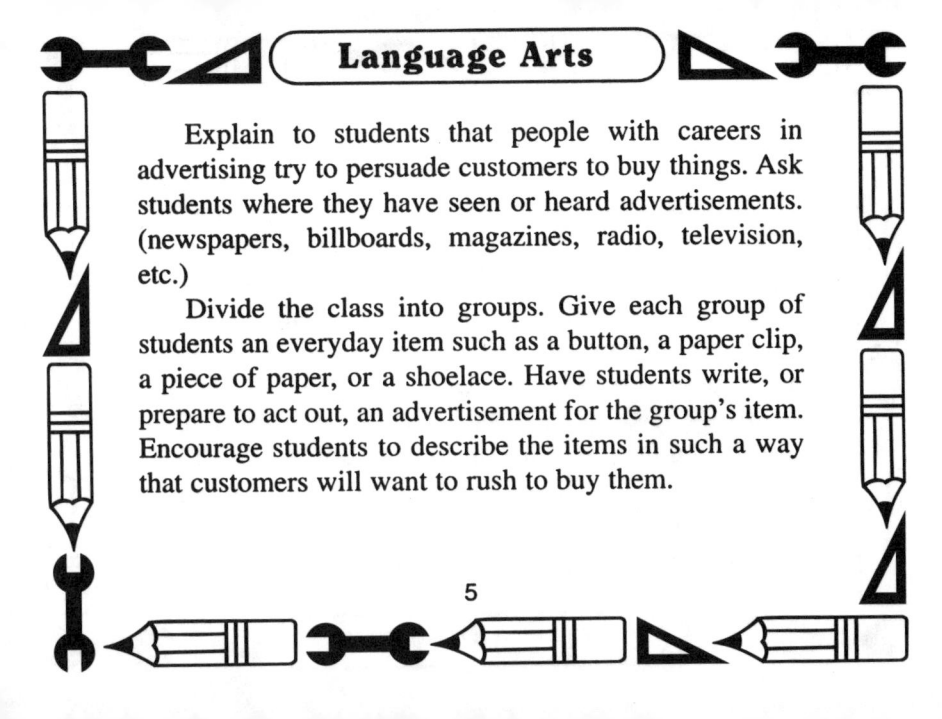

Language Arts

Explain to students that people with careers in advertising try to persuade customers to buy things. Ask students where they have seen or heard advertisements. (newspapers, billboards, magazines, radio, television, etc.)

Divide the class into groups. Give each group of students an everyday item such as a button, a paper clip, a piece of paper, or a shoelace. Have students write, or prepare to act out, an advertisement for the group's item. Encourage students to describe the items in such a way that customers will want to rush to buy them.

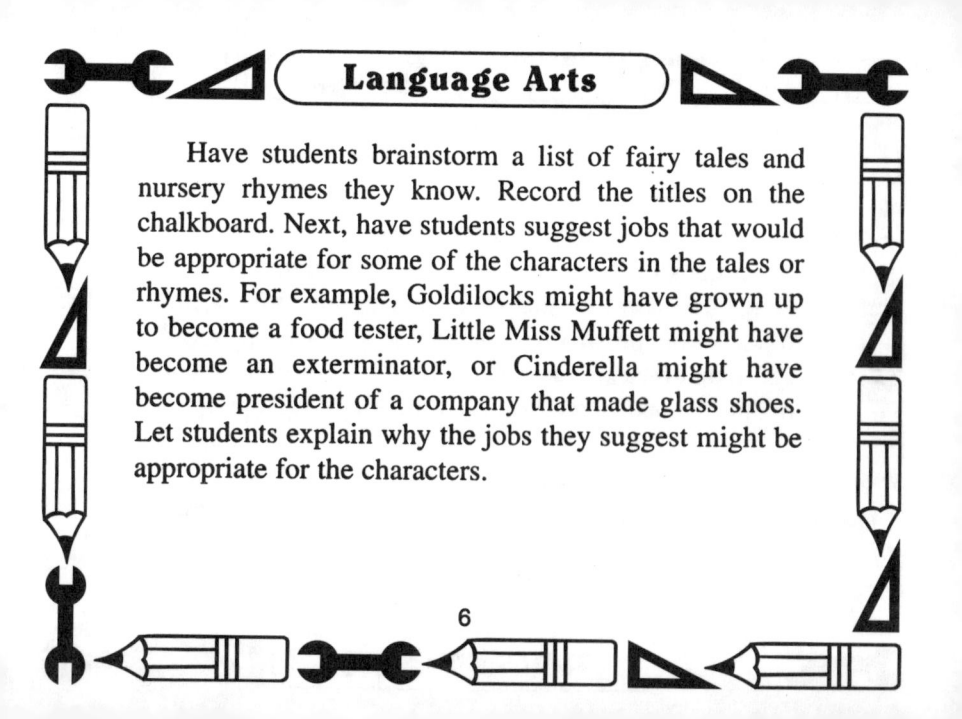

Language Arts

Have students brainstorm a list of fairy tales and nursery rhymes they know. Record the titles on the chalkboard. Next, have students suggest jobs that would be appropriate for some of the characters in the tales or rhymes. For example, Goldilocks might have grown up to become a food tester, Little Miss Muffett might have become an exterminator, or Cinderella might have become president of a company that made glass shoes. Let students explain why the jobs they suggest might be appropriate for the characters.

Language Arts

Have students brainstorm careers that involve working with food. Explain what a caterer is, then read the following aloud: *You love being a caterer. As a caterer you make large amounts of food for parties. You are working on your biggest job ever, making food for one hundred people. First, you look into the oven and see that your cheese puffs have burned! Then your helper calls to say he is unable to come to work. Just as you are leaving for the big party, where you plan to serve shrimp for a hundred people, you get a phone call saying some of the guests can't eat shrimp! What will you do?*

Have students tell or write their solutions to these catering problems. Next, have students brainstorm and suggest solutions for problems that might arise in other careers.

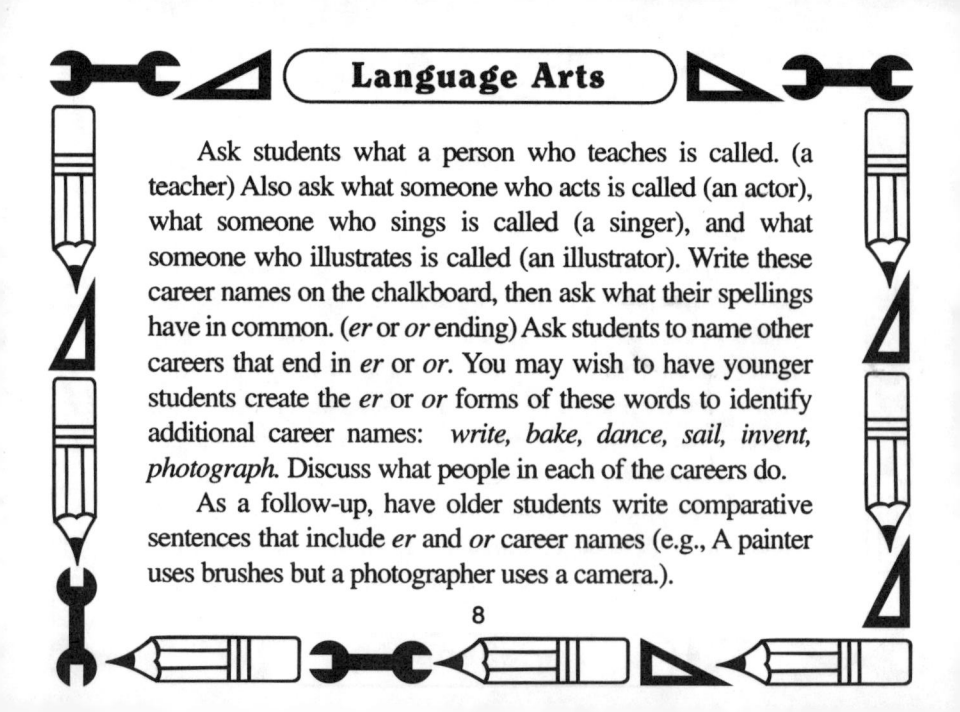

Language Arts

Ask students what a person who teaches is called. (a teacher) Also ask what someone who acts is called (an actor), what someone who sings is called (a singer), and what someone who illustrates is called (an illustrator). Write these career names on the chalkboard, then ask what their spellings have in common. (*er* or *or* ending) Ask students to name other careers that end in *er* or *or*. You may wish to have younger students create the *er* or *or* forms of these words to identify additional career names: *write, bake, dance, sail, invent, photograph*. Discuss what people in each of the careers do.

As a follow-up, have older students write comparative sentences that include *er* and *or* career names (e.g., A painter uses brushes but a photographer uses a camera.).

Language Arts

Write the following question on the chalkboard several times: *When am I going to use ___?* Then fill the blanks with the subject areas students study each week (science, math, language arts, etc.). Help students brainstorm a list of careers that involve knowing the information and skills taught in each subject area. Write students' responses on the board. For example, under the language arts heading you might list *writer, reporter, editor, poet,* and *attorney.* Encourage students to work beyond their first thoughts. For example, any person who writes reports, such as a police officer or a nurse, uses language arts skills.

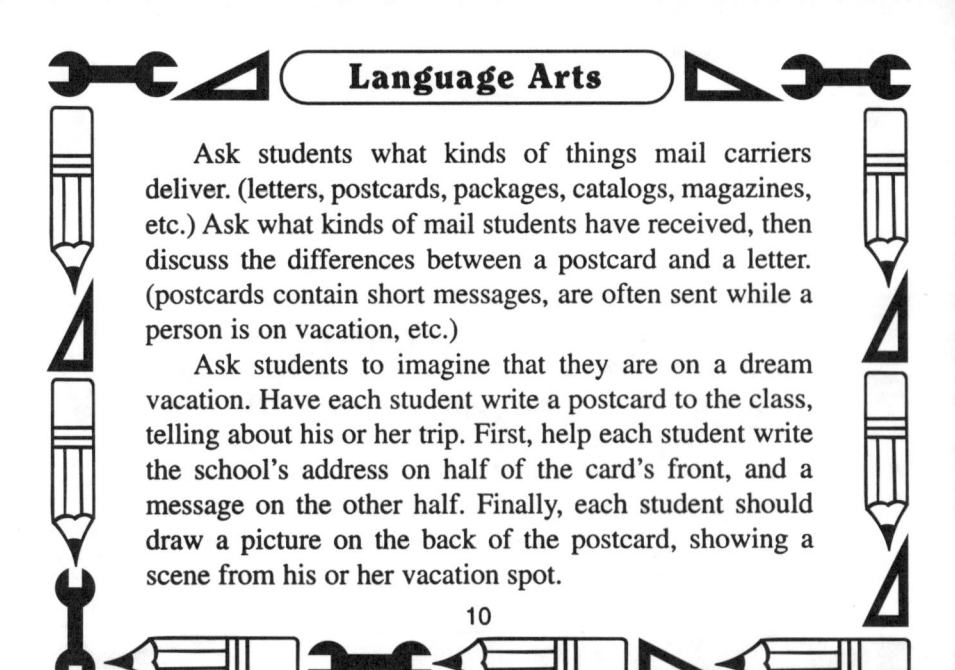

Language Arts

Ask students what kinds of things mail carriers deliver. (letters, postcards, packages, catalogs, magazines, etc.) Ask what kinds of mail students have received, then discuss the differences between a postcard and a letter. (postcards contain short messages, are often sent while a person is on vacation, etc.)

Ask students to imagine that they are on a dream vacation. Have each student write a postcard to the class, telling about his or her trip. First, help each student write the school's address on half of the card's front, and a message on the other half. Finally, each student should draw a picture on the back of the postcard, showing a scene from his or her vacation spot.

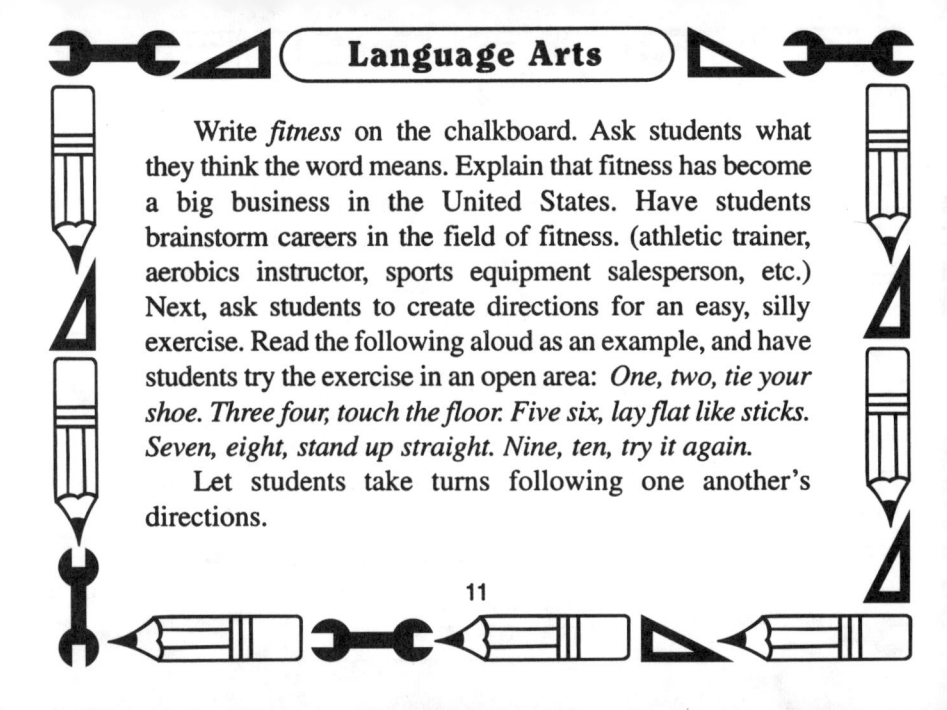

Language Arts

Write *fitness* on the chalkboard. Ask students what they think the word means. Explain that fitness has become a big business in the United States. Have students brainstorm careers in the field of fitness. (athletic trainer, aerobics instructor, sports equipment salesperson, etc.) Next, ask students to create directions for an easy, silly exercise. Read the following aloud as an example, and have students try the exercise in an open area: *One, two, tie your shoe. Three four, touch the floor. Five six, lay flat like sticks. Seven, eight, stand up straight. Nine, ten, try it again.*

Let students take turns following one another's directions.

Language Arts

Explain to students that authors are people who make a living by writing. Ask what kinds of things authors write. (poems, news articles, stories, nonfiction books, etc.) Discuss the fact that authors who write stories try to develop interesting titles for them. Ask students what story titles should do (e.g., tell a reader something about the book, capture a reader's attention). Read aloud the titles of several short storybooks students have not read. Ask students what they think the stories are about and whether or not the titles sound interesting. Read the stories aloud, or have students read them in groups. Have students check their predictions about the stories. Finally, ask students to develop new, interesting titles for them.

Language Arts

Ask students to think of some careers that are associated with clothing. (manufacturing, designing, selling, advertising, etc.) Explain that fashion designers, clothing manufacturers, and tailors design and make clothing.

Point out that some terms, such as *bookcase* or *bedroom,* are made up of two smaller words. Have students brainstorm clothing-related compound words (e.g., turtleneck, shoelace, earmuffs, wristwatch, earring, necktie, headband, sweatshirt, sweatpants, necklace). Then have students break into groups and work together to draw a person wearing many items of clothing with compound names. Ask students to label the items correctly.

Language Arts

Have each student write a poem about a career that interests him or her. The poem should show what the student knows about the career. Copy the following example onto the chalkboard, then have a volunteer read it aloud:

If I were a farmer,
I'd work outside all day.
I'd milk the cows, and feed the pigs,
and give the horses hay.

Have students use this poem as a model to write their own poems that begin with "If I were a . . ." You may wish to work with younger students to compose several group poems.

Language Arts

Ask students what it means to interview someone. (to ask the person questions) Tell students that they are going to interview people who work at the school. Explain that each student is to find out as much as possible about the person's job. After stressing the importance of asking good questions during an interview, assign a member of the school's staff to each pair of students. Have students write five to ten career-related questions to ask the people. Check the students' questions, then set up times and places for the interviews. When the interviews have been completed, have each student write a few sentences or give a brief oral presentation to summarize what he or she learned.

Language Arts

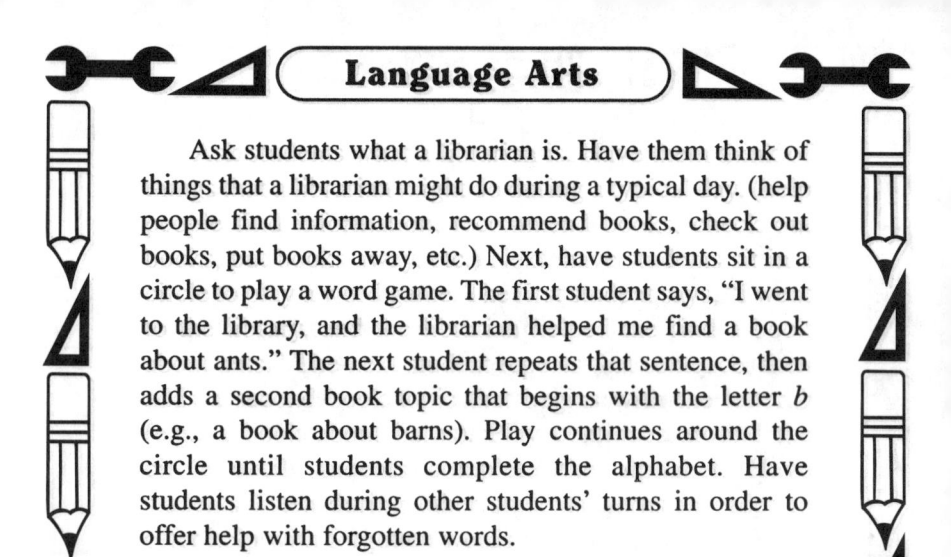

Ask students what a librarian is. Have them think of things that a librarian might do during a typical day. (help people find information, recommend books, check out books, put books away, etc.) Next, have students sit in a circle to play a word game. The first student says, "I went to the library, and the librarian helped me find a book about ants." The next student repeats that sentence, then adds a second book topic that begins with the letter *b* (e.g., a book about barns). Play continues around the circle until students complete the alphabet. Have students listen during other students' turns in order to offer help with forgotten words.

Language Arts

Work with students to compare and contrast careers by using Venn diagrams. As an example, draw two overlapping circles on the chalkboard. Write *fire fighters* in one circle and *police officers* in the other. Have students suggest ways the two careers are alike and different. Write similarities in the overlapping parts of the circles. Write differences inside the appropriate circles but outside of the overlapping areas. See the example below.

Now divide the class into small groups. Have each group choose two more careers and create a Venn diagram similar to the one you modeled.

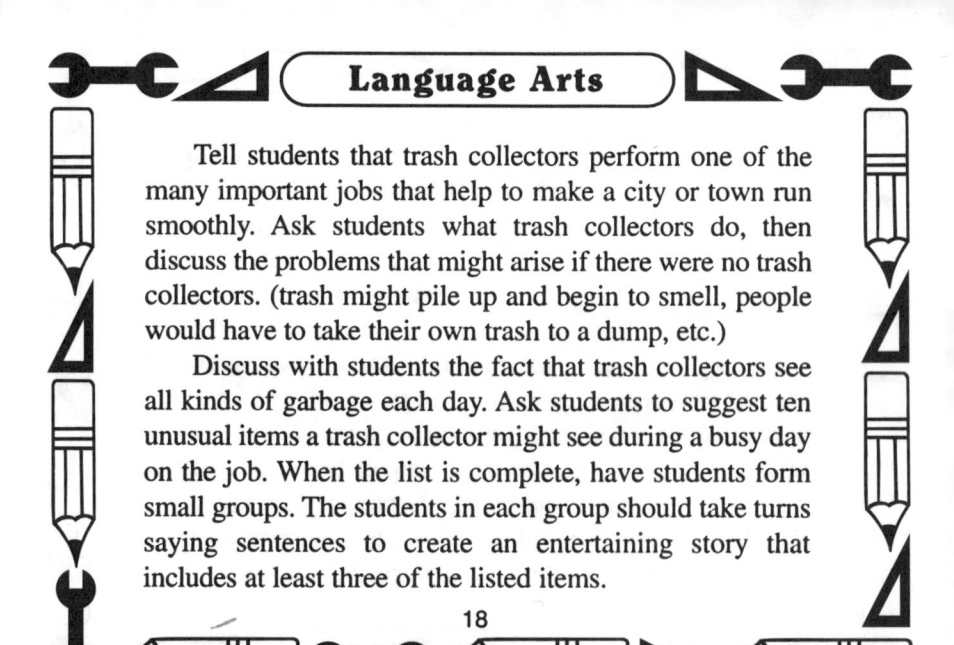

Language Arts

Tell students that trash collectors perform one of the many important jobs that help to make a city or town run smoothly. Ask students what trash collectors do, then discuss the problems that might arise if there were no trash collectors. (trash might pile up and begin to smell, people would have to take their own trash to a dump, etc.)

Discuss with students the fact that trash collectors see all kinds of garbage each day. Ask students to suggest ten unusual items a trash collector might see during a busy day on the job. When the list is complete, have students form small groups. The students in each group should take turns saying sentences to create an entertaining story that includes at least three of the listed items.

Language Arts

Ask students what waiters and waitresses do. (serve food and drinks) Then copy the following sentences onto the chalkboard: *Are you ready to order? Here is your menu. Wow, this plate is hot!* Ask student volunteers to read the sentences aloud. Talk about how each sentence's end punctuation affects the way it is read. Finally, divide students into pairs. Have each pair write three more sentences a waiter, a waitress, or a restaurant customer might say. One should be interrogative, one should be declarative, and one should be exclamatory. Then have students act out a situation in which their sentences might be said. Students who are watching should identify what end punctuation would appear at the end of each sentence.

Language Arts

Write the following sentences on large strips of paper:

The chef took the pie out of the oven.
The gardener put the tree into the ground.
The bus driver stopped to pick up a student.
The student stepped off the bus.
The gardener pushed down the mud around the tree trunk.
The chef baked the pie.
The student rode on the bus.
The chef measured the ingredients.
The gardener dug a hole.

Have students identify which sentences belong together, then ask them to put each set of three sentences in the correct order. Finally, have each student write and sequence three sentences about another career.

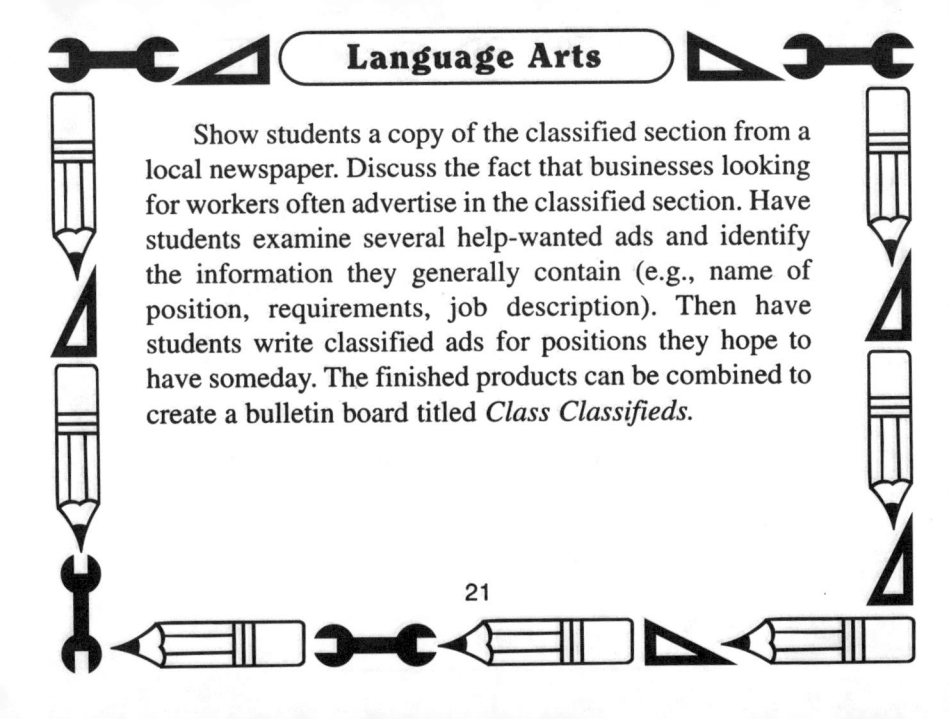

Language Arts

Show students a copy of the classified section from a local newspaper. Discuss the fact that businesses looking for workers often advertise in the classified section. Have students examine several help-wanted ads and identify the information they generally contain (e.g., name of position, requirements, job description). Then have students write classified ads for positions they hope to have someday. The finished products can be combined to create a bulletin board titled *Class Classifieds*.

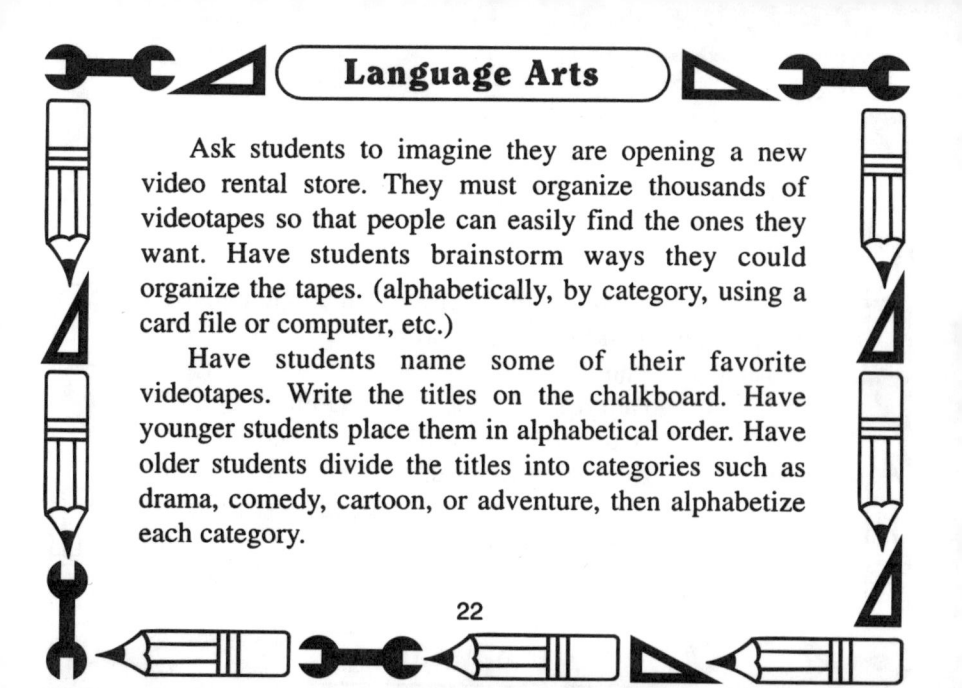

Language Arts

Ask students to imagine they are opening a new video rental store. They must organize thousands of videotapes so that people can easily find the ones they want. Have students brainstorm ways they could organize the tapes. (alphabetically, by category, using a card file or computer, etc.)

Have students name some of their favorite videotapes. Write the titles on the chalkboard. Have younger students place them in alphabetical order. Have older students divide the titles into categories such as drama, comedy, cartoon, or adventure, then alphabetize each category.

Language Arts

Discuss with students the fact that some people have sports-related careers. Have students brainstorm some jobs that involve sports. (professional athletics, sports writing, manufacturing or selling athletic equipment, sports announcing, etc.) Now ask each student to think about his or her favorite sport and write action words that are related to that sport (e.g., baseball—hit, swing, catch, slide). Each younger student can write his or her list inside a shape that is related to the sport, such as a baseball bat, a hockey puck, or a football. Have older students write action poems that include some of the verbs they listed. Display students' completed work on a bulletin board.

Language Arts

Explain to students that some authors make up stories, and that made-up stories are called fiction. Other authors write about real people or events. Explain that this writing is called nonfiction. Ask students to identify books with the following titles as either fiction or nonfiction: *George Washington and His Life* (nonfiction), *Toby the Talking Tooth* (fiction), *The Day the World Turned Purple* (fiction), *All About Monkeys* (nonfiction), *How to Plant a Garden* (nonfiction). Then have each student create two book covers for books they might like to write someday. One book should have a nonfiction title and the other should have a fiction title. Students should also include their names and appropriate artwork on the covers.

Language Arts

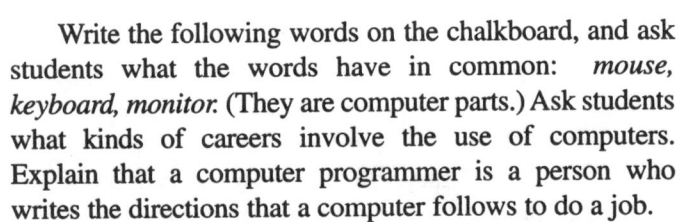

Write the following words on the chalkboard, and ask students what the words have in common: *mouse, keyboard, monitor.* (They are computer parts.) Ask students what kinds of careers involve the use of computers. Explain that a computer programmer is a person who writes the directions that a computer follows to do a job.

Tell (remind) students what a syllable is, then have students read the three words on the chalkboard and identify the number of syllables in each. Younger students may clap along as they say a word to identify its syllables. Finally, have students work in groups to list other careers, and name 1-, 2-, and 3-syllable words that are related to those careers.

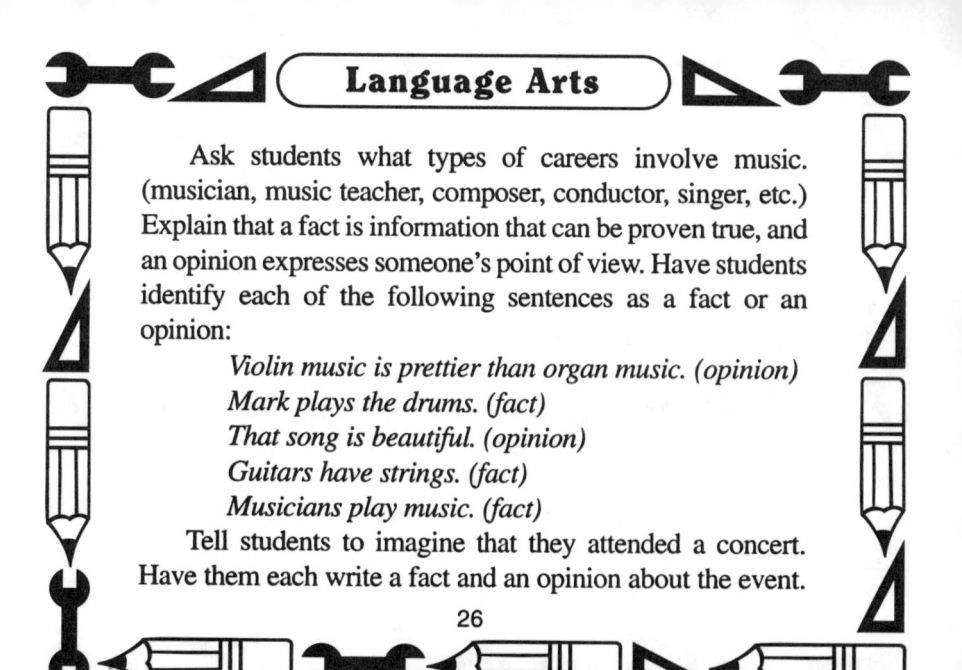

Language Arts

Ask students what types of careers involve music. (musician, music teacher, composer, conductor, singer, etc.) Explain that a fact is information that can be proven true, and an opinion expresses someone's point of view. Have students identify each of the following sentences as a fact or an opinion:

Violin music is prettier than organ music. (opinion)
Mark plays the drums. (fact)
That song is beautiful. (opinion)
Guitars have strings. (fact)
Musicians play music. (fact)

Tell students to imagine that they attended a concert. Have them each write a fact and an opinion about the event.

Language Arts

Discuss with students the fact that the ability to speak well is an important skill in many careers. Ask students why this ability would be important to the following people: teacher, newscaster, attorney, politician (president). Then talk about what makes a speaker effective. (clear speaking voice, well prepared, makes eye contact with audience members, etc.)

As a follow-up, have each student speak in front of the class. A student may demonstrate a skill, explain a concept, express an opinion, recite a poem, etc. Give students time to prepare, then have them present their speeches to the class. You may want to tell the student audience that careful listening is an important skill, too.

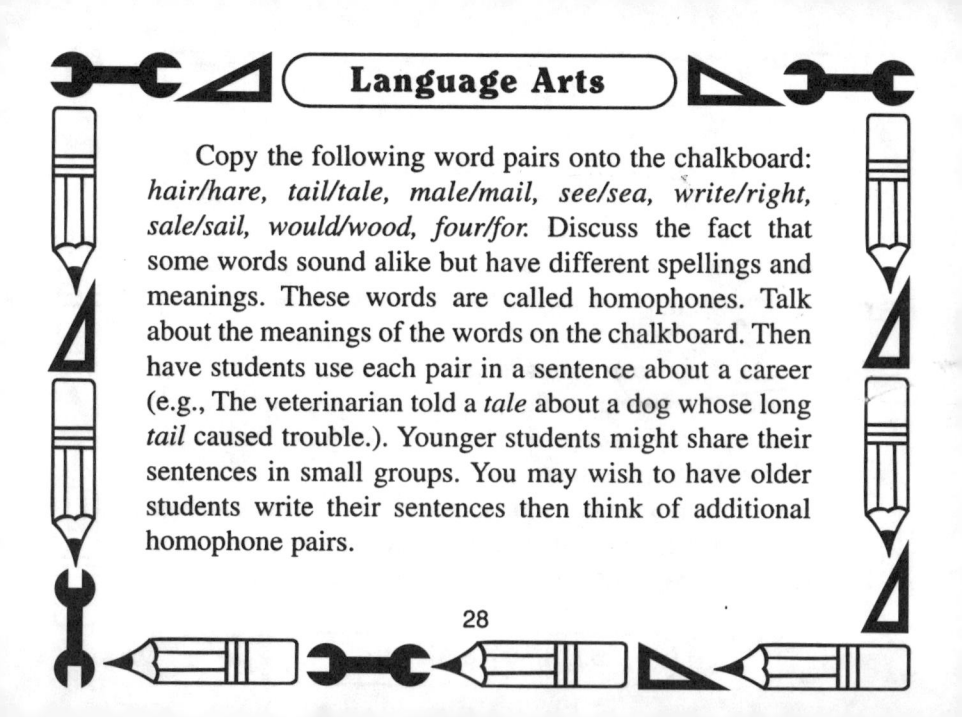

Language Arts

Copy the following word pairs onto the chalkboard: *hair/hare, tail/tale, male/mail, see/sea, write/right, sale/sail, would/wood, four/for.* Discuss the fact that some words sound alike but have different spellings and meanings. These words are called homophones. Talk about the meanings of the words on the chalkboard. Then have students use each pair in a sentence about a career (e.g., The veterinarian told a *tale* about a dog whose long *tail* caused trouble.). Younger students might share their sentences in small groups. You may wish to have older students write their sentences then think of additional homophone pairs.

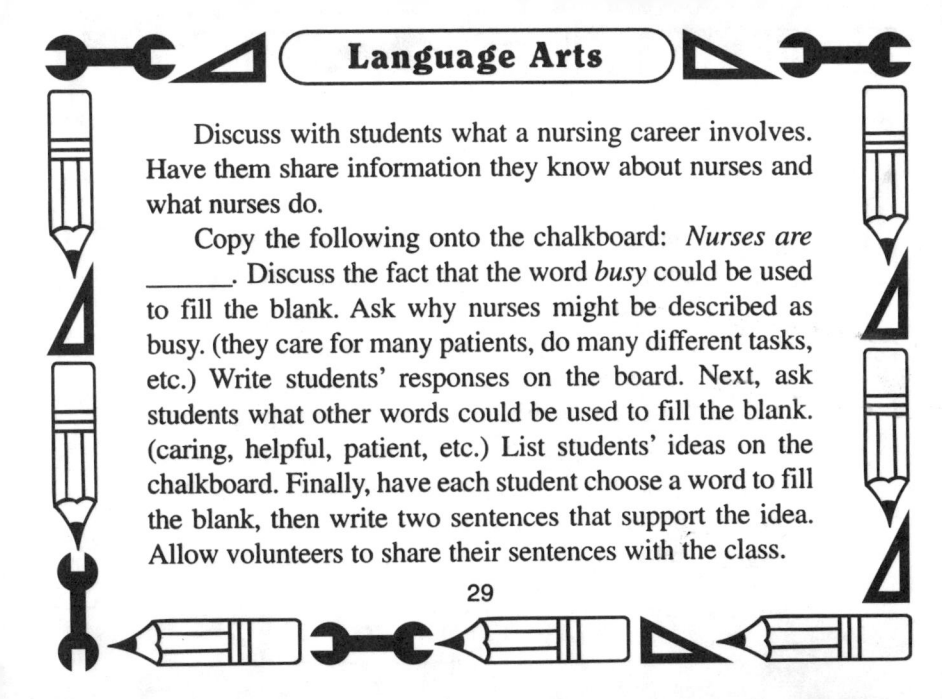

Language Arts

Discuss with students what a nursing career involves. Have them share information they know about nurses and what nurses do.

Copy the following onto the chalkboard: *Nurses are* _____. Discuss the fact that the word *busy* could be used to fill the blank. Ask why nurses might be described as busy. (they care for many patients, do many different tasks, etc.) Write students' responses on the board. Next, ask students what other words could be used to fill the blank. (caring, helpful, patient, etc.) List students' ideas on the chalkboard. Finally, have each student choose a word to fill the blank, then write two sentences that support the idea. Allow volunteers to share their sentences with the class.

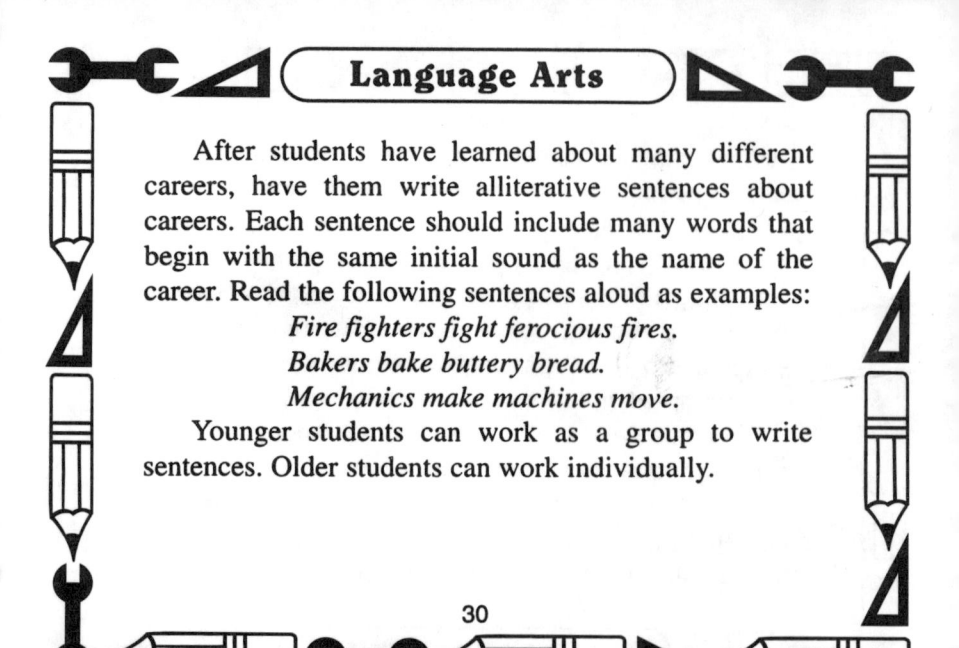

Language Arts

After students have learned about many different careers, have them write alliterative sentences about careers. Each sentence should include many words that begin with the same initial sound as the name of the career. Read the following sentences aloud as examples:

Fire fighters fight ferocious fires.
Bakers bake buttery bread.
Mechanics make machines move.

Younger students can work as a group to write sentences. Older students can work individually.

Language Arts

Copy the following sentences onto the chalkboard: *Some people work <u>in high places</u>. Some people work <u>in low places</u>.* Have students identify people with jobs in high places (pilot, window washer, astronaut, etc.) and people with jobs in low places (miner, deep-sea diver, subway worker, etc.). Now list the following pairs on the chalkboard: inside/outside, alone/in a group, in the city/in the country, with children/with adults. Have students replace the underlined words on the board with one of the new pairs, then identify jobs that fit their new categories.

As a follow-up, each student might illustrate the careers that support one of the pairs of sentences.

Language Arts

Explain to students that the first letters in the lines of an acrostic spell a word. Copy the following poem onto the chalkboard as an example:

*P*ilots
*I*n their cockpits,
*L*anding planes
*O*r soaring over clouds,
*T*ake travelers to faraway places.

Have each student choose another career and create an acrostic that tells something about that career. Younger students can list just one or two words on each line of their poems. Older students can choose longer career names.

Language Arts

Have students play "Guess My Career." Read these characteristics of a career while students try to guess the career you have in mind:

1. I know a great deal about animals.
2. I help to keep animals healthy.
3. You can bring your pets to me when they are sick.
4. I am a doctor for animals. (veterinarian)

Allow students to work in groups to repeat the activity for other careers. Another way to play is to have one student think of a career and allow other students to ask yes or no questions until they figure out what the career is.

Language Arts

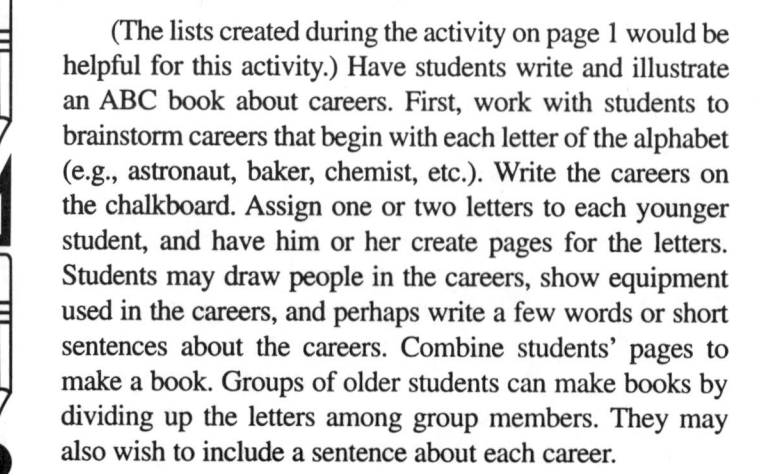

(The lists created during the activity on page 1 would be helpful for this activity.) Have students write and illustrate an ABC book about careers. First, work with students to brainstorm careers that begin with each letter of the alphabet (e.g., astronaut, baker, chemist, etc.). Write the careers on the chalkboard. Assign one or two letters to each younger student, and have him or her create pages for the letters. Students may draw people in the careers, show equipment used in the careers, and perhaps write a few words or short sentences about the careers. Combine students' pages to make a book. Groups of older students can make books by dividing up the letters among group members. They may also wish to include a sentence about each career.

Language Arts

Write the following poem verses on the chalkboard. Work with students to write similar verses about other careers.

Baker, baker, what do you make?
I make goodies like cookies and cake.

Dentist, dentist, what do you do?
I take care of your teeth for you.

Students may enjoy reciting the completed verses together and adding appropriate motions to them. For example, they might rub their stomachs during the verse about a baker, or pretend to brush their teeth during the verse about a dentist.

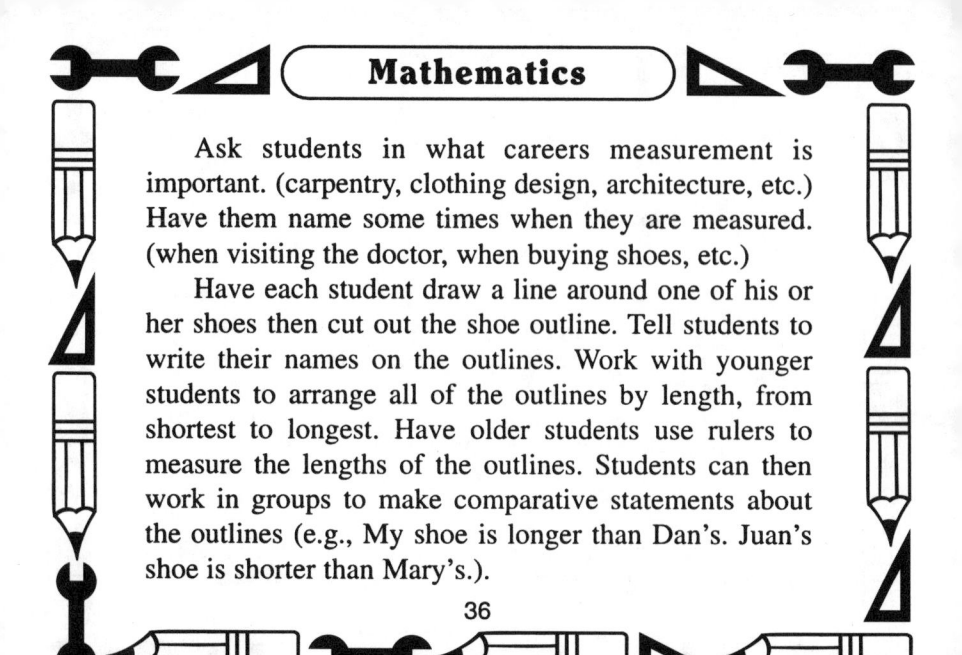

Mathematics

Ask students in what careers measurement is important. (carpentry, clothing design, architecture, etc.) Have them name some times when they are measured. (when visiting the doctor, when buying shoes, etc.)

Have each student draw a line around one of his or her shoes then cut out the shoe outline. Tell students to write their names on the outlines. Work with younger students to arrange all of the outlines by length, from shortest to longest. Have older students use rulers to measure the lengths of the outlines. Students can then work in groups to make comparative statements about the outlines (e.g., My shoe is longer than Dan's. Juan's shoe is shorter than Mary's.).

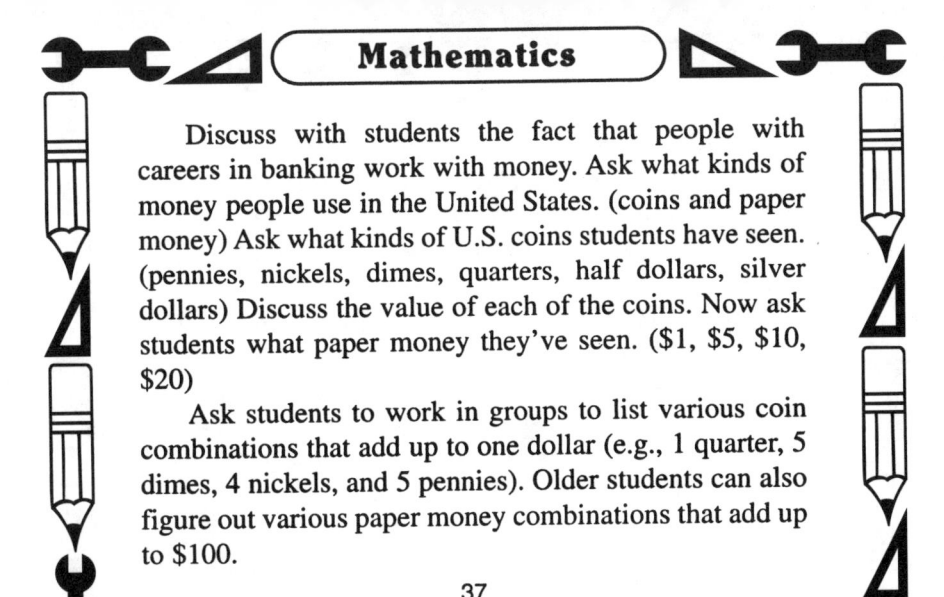

Mathematics

Discuss with students the fact that people with careers in banking work with money. Ask what kinds of money people use in the United States. (coins and paper money) Ask what kinds of U.S. coins students have seen. (pennies, nickels, dimes, quarters, half dollars, silver dollars) Discuss the value of each of the coins. Now ask students what paper money they've seen. ($1, $5, $10, $20)

Ask students to work in groups to list various coin combinations that add up to one dollar (e.g., 1 quarter, 5 dimes, 4 nickels, and 5 pennies). Older students can also figure out various paper money combinations that add up to $100.

Mathematics

Ask students what a baker does. (creates baked goods)
Discuss the fact that baked goods are often purchased by the
dozen. Ask students if they know how many items are in a
dozen. (12) Next, have students solve the following word
problems. You may wish to give younger students cereal *o*'s
which they can use as counters that represent donuts.

1. How many rolls are in a half-dozen? (6)
2. If a person needs 24 cupcakes, how many dozen should he
   or she buy? (2)
3. How many donuts are in a dozen and a half? (18)
4. If a roll costs 10¢, how much will a dozen rolls cost? ($1.20)

Have students create word problems involving baked goods
and dozens, then have them exchange problems and solve them.

Mathematics

Ask students what photographers do. (take and sometimes develop photographs) Give each student a photocopy of a page that contains outlines of 3 squares, 2 circles, 1 rectangle, and 4 triangles. Have students cut out the shapes while you prepare a set for yourself. Put masking tape loops on the backs of the shapes in your set, then use the shapes to create a design on the chalkboard. Tell students to imagine they are photographers. Have them use their shapes to create a "photograph" (copy) of the design you've made on the chalkboard. When students have finished, have them work in pairs to create and copy new designs with the shapes.

Mathematics

Ask students what is sold in hardware stores. (nails, tools, lumber, etc.) Have students imagine that they work in a hardware store. Explain that they are responsible for ordering items. To do this, they must know how many of each item the store needs and how many the store has in stock. Copy the following chart onto the chalkboard:

item	# needed	# in stock	# to order
bolts	10	7	
hammers	5	1	
rakes	15		5

Have students fill in the missing information and make up additional rows. Younger students might use bolts or other hardware items as counters during the activity.

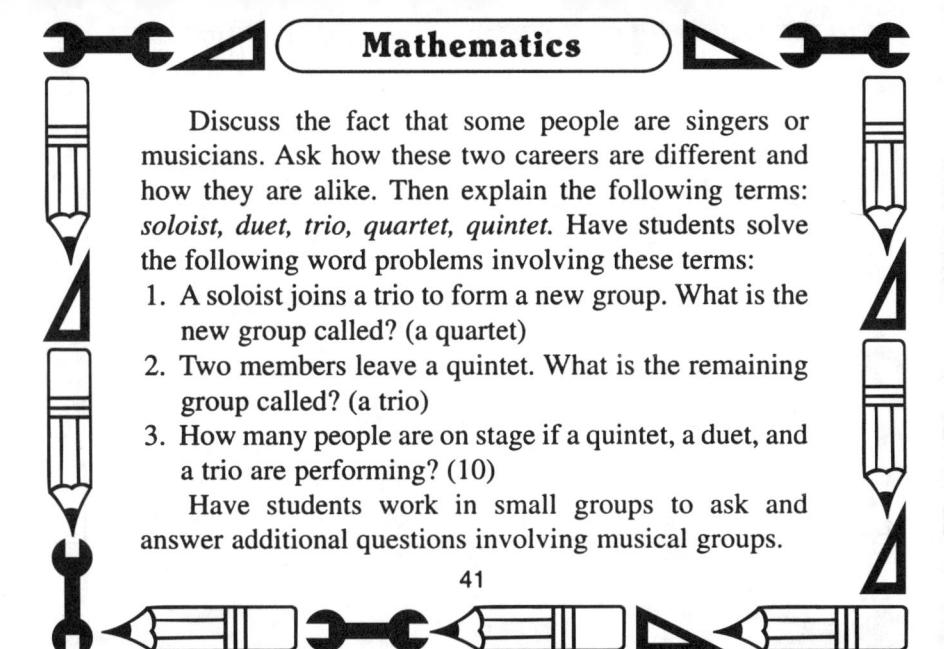

Mathematics

Discuss the fact that some people are singers or musicians. Ask how these two careers are different and how they are alike. Then explain the following terms: *soloist, duet, trio, quartet, quintet.* Have students solve the following word problems involving these terms:
1. A soloist joins a trio to form a new group. What is the new group called? (a quartet)
2. Two members leave a quintet. What is the remaining group called? (a trio)
3. How many people are on stage if a quintet, a duet, and a trio are performing? (10)

Have students work in small groups to ask and answer additional questions involving musical groups.

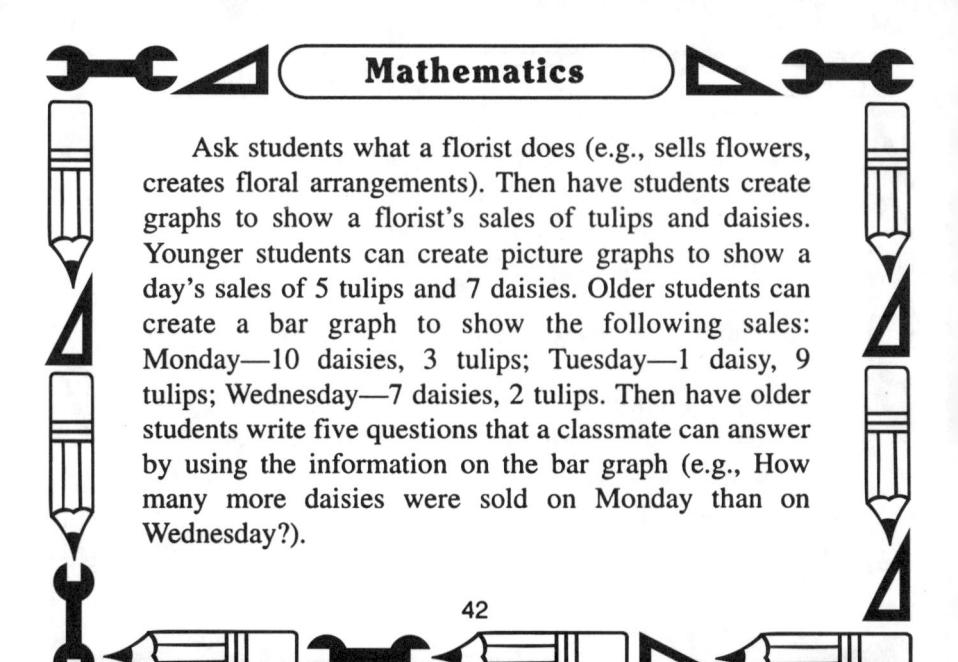

Mathematics

Ask students what a florist does (e.g., sells flowers, creates floral arrangements). Then have students create graphs to show a florist's sales of tulips and daisies. Younger students can create picture graphs to show a day's sales of 5 tulips and 7 daisies. Older students can create a bar graph to show the following sales: Monday—10 daisies, 3 tulips; Tuesday—1 daisy, 9 tulips; Wednesday—7 daisies, 2 tulips. Then have older students write five questions that a classmate can answer by using the information on the bar graph (e.g., How many more daisies were sold on Monday than on Wednesday?).

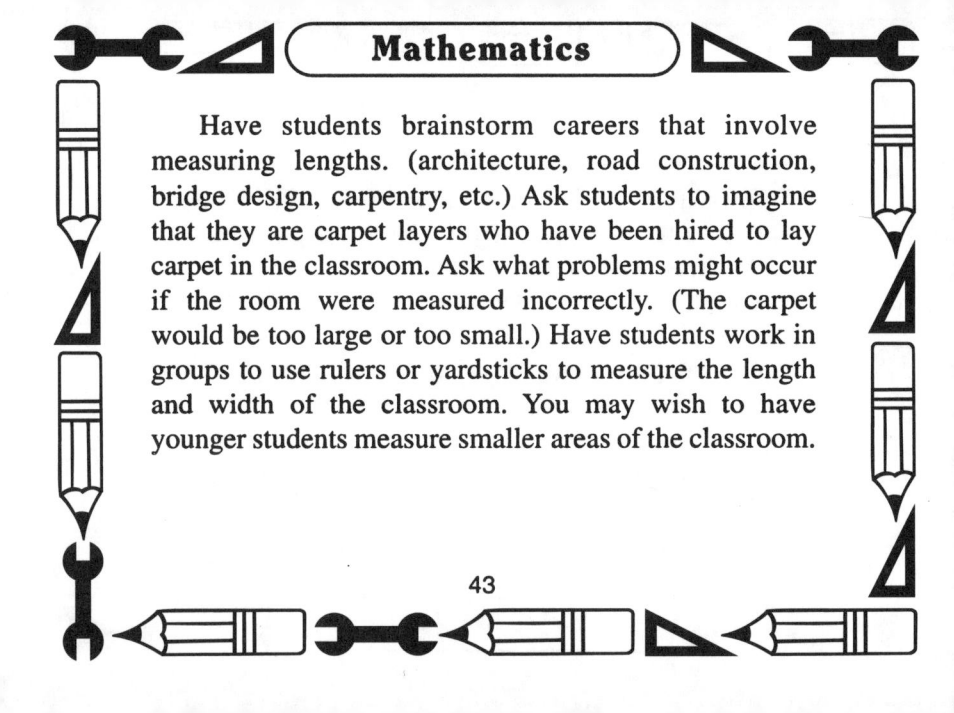

Mathematics

Have students brainstorm careers that involve measuring lengths. (architecture, road construction, bridge design, carpentry, etc.) Ask students to imagine that they are carpet layers who have been hired to lay carpet in the classroom. Ask what problems might occur if the room were measured incorrectly. (The carpet would be too large or too small.) Have students work in groups to use rulers or yardsticks to measure the length and width of the classroom. You may wish to have younger students measure smaller areas of the classroom.

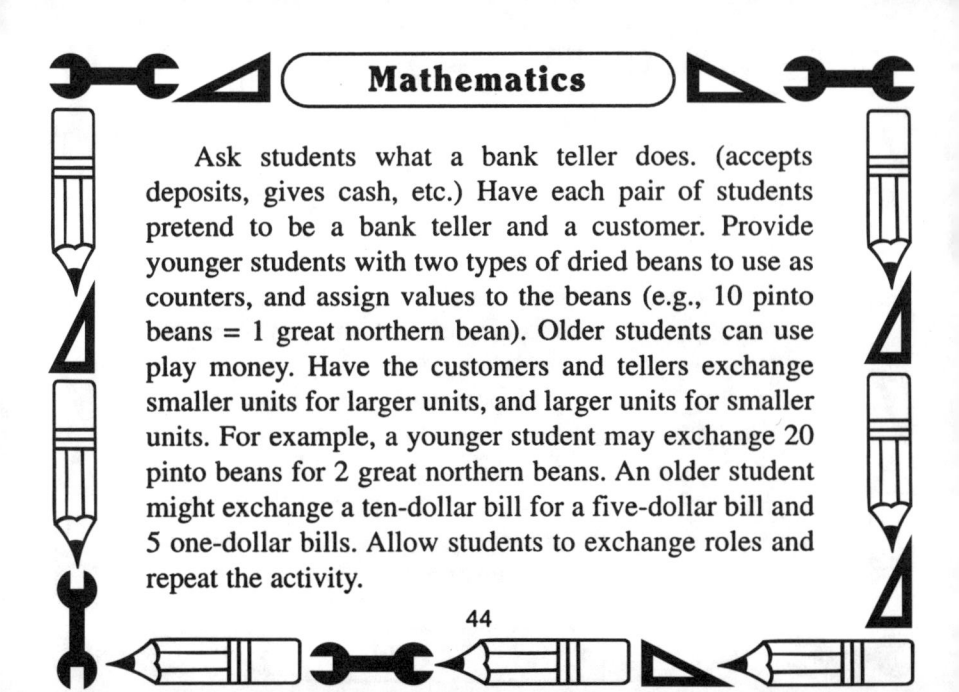

Mathematics

Ask students what a bank teller does. (accepts deposits, gives cash, etc.) Have each pair of students pretend to be a bank teller and a customer. Provide younger students with two types of dried beans to use as counters, and assign values to the beans (e.g., 10 pinto beans = 1 great northern bean). Older students can use play money. Have the customers and tellers exchange smaller units for larger units, and larger units for smaller units. For example, a younger student may exchange 20 pinto beans for 2 great northern beans. An older student might exchange a ten-dollar bill for a five-dollar bill and 5 one-dollar bills. Allow students to exchange roles and repeat the activity.

Mathematics

Explain to students that business owners must know how much money they are spending and how much they are earning. Have students act as owners as they solve the following problems about a lemonade stand: *If a cup costs 3¢ and the lemonade to fill a cup costs 4¢, what is the actual cost of a cup of lemonade? (7¢) What is the least the owner can charge for a cup of lemonade and make money? (8¢) If an owner charges 10¢ for each cup, how much money would he or she make on each cup? (3¢) on ten cups? (30¢)*

Have student "owners" follow up by discussing how price, weather, and location might affect the sales of a lemonade stand.

Mathematics

Ask students what a jeweler does. (sells, repairs, and makes jewelry) Copy this sales information onto the chalkboard: *A jeweler sells the following number of rings during a week: Monday–4, Tuesday–6, Wednesday–7, Thursday–1, Friday–2.* Then ask students the following questions:

1. How many rings did the jeweler sell during the week? (20)
2. On which day did the jeweler sell the most rings? (Wednesday)
3. How many more rings did the jeweler sell on Monday than on Thursday? (3)

Have students create and solve other problems based on the information about the jeweler.

Mathematics

Have students bring in empty two-liter plastic soft drink bottles to be used as "bowling pins." You will also need several soccer balls (or balls of a similar size).

Discuss with students the fact that some people play professional sports as a career. Talk about how numbers are important in sports. (scores, distances, salaries, etc.) Then tell students that they are going to be professional bowlers for a day. Have groups of three students set up pins on the playground or in the gym. Have students take turns bowling, setting up pins, and keeping score. Younger students can add up the number of pins knocked down each time. Older students can set values for the pins each round. For example, during the ninth round each pin might be worth nine points.

Mathematics

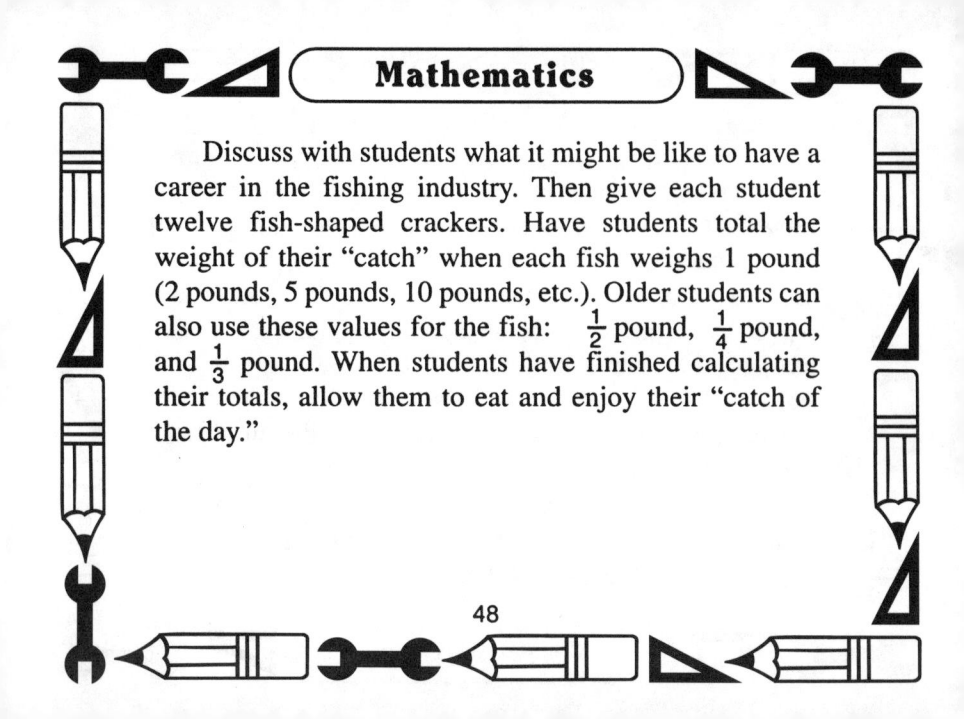

Discuss with students what it might be like to have a career in the fishing industry. Then give each student twelve fish-shaped crackers. Have students total the weight of their "catch" when each fish weighs 1 pound (2 pounds, 5 pounds, 10 pounds, etc.). Older students can also use these values for the fish: $\frac{1}{2}$ pound, $\frac{1}{4}$ pound, and $\frac{1}{3}$ pound. When students have finished calculating their totals, allow them to eat and enjoy their "catch of the day."

Mathematics

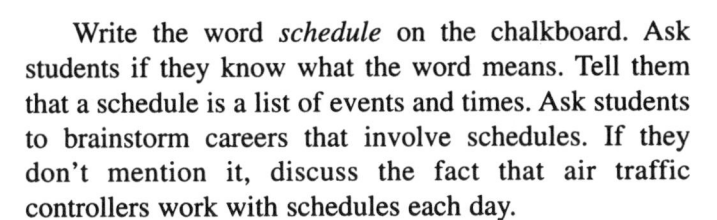

Write the word *schedule* on the chalkboard. Ask students if they know what the word means. Tell them that a schedule is a list of events and times. Ask students to brainstorm careers that involve schedules. If they don't mention it, discuss the fact that air traffic controllers work with schedules each day.

Tell students that an airplane leaves an airport at 9 a.m. Show younger students a moveable clock face, and ask what time the plane will land if it is a one-hour (2-hour, 3-hour, 4-hour, etc.) flight. Work with older students to write a 12-hour schedule for the plane if it makes two-hour flights and stays on the ground for fifteen minutes between each flight.

Mathematics

Students will need graph paper to complete this activity. Prepare and copy a grid with $\frac{1}{2}$" squares for younger students.

Discuss with students the fact that a pattern is a design that repeats itself. Explain that checkered cloth, for example, follows a pattern. Have students look around the room to find patterns (e.g., floor tiles). Then give each student a piece of graph paper. Tell students to imagine that they are bricklayers who are working with two colors of brick to create a wall. Have them each use two crayons or markers and the graph paper to create a pattern for the wall. Encourage students to create unique patterns that repeat themselves in some way.

Mathematics

Ask students to name some of the jobs secretaries do. (file, answer phones, type on computers, etc.) Explain that a company has four secretaries and each works at a different speed. Copy the following information onto the chalkboard: *Carol types 4 letters in an hour; Jim types 5 letters in an hour; Keshia types 6 letters in an hour; Maria types 7 letters in an hour.*

Ask students how many letters Keshia could type in 2 hours. (12) How many letters could Carol type in 2 hours? (8) Give older students practice with division by asking questions such as: *How long would it take Jim to type 25 letters?* (5 hours) Have students ask one another additional questions based on the information on the chalkboard.

Mathematics

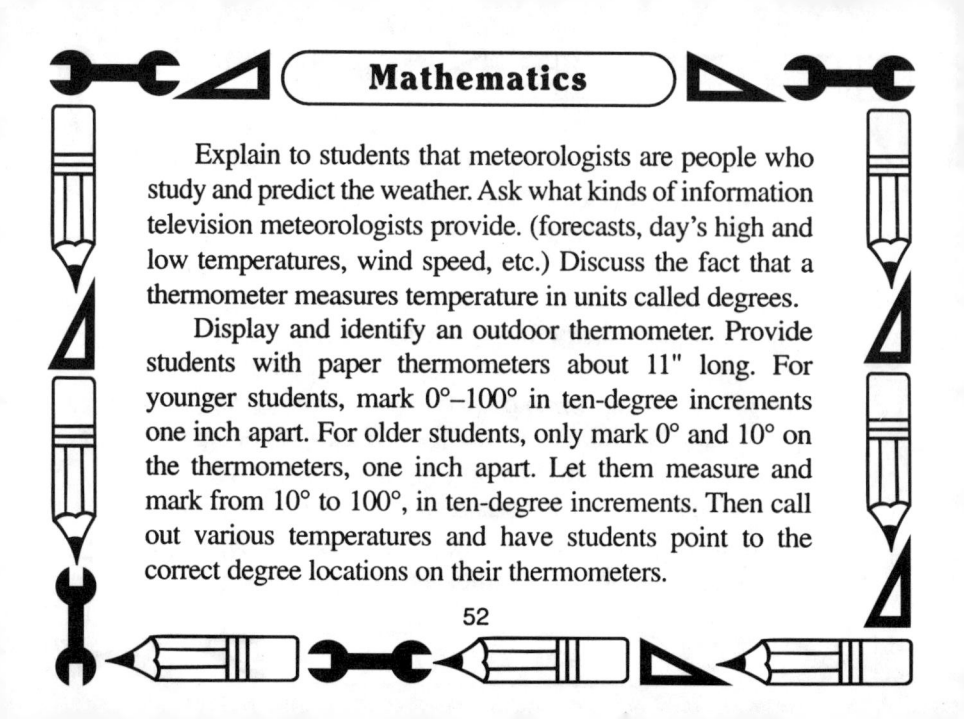

Explain to students that meteorologists are people who study and predict the weather. Ask what kinds of information television meteorologists provide. (forecasts, day's high and low temperatures, wind speed, etc.) Discuss the fact that a thermometer measures temperature in units called degrees.

Display and identify an outdoor thermometer. Provide students with paper thermometers about 11" long. For younger students, mark 0°–100° in ten-degree increments one inch apart. For older students, only mark 0° and 10° on the thermometers, one inch apart. Let them measure and mark from 10° to 100°, in ten-degree increments. Then call out various temperatures and have students point to the correct degree locations on their thermometers.

Mathematics

Discuss with students the fact that some people have careers in the restaurant business. Ask students if they've ever eaten in a pizza restaurant. Then have each student draw three large circles on a sheet of paper. Tell students that the circles are pizzas. Ask students to draw lines on the circles to show how to cut a pizza into two, four, and eight equal pieces. Discuss the fractions students' drawings show (halves, fourths, eighths). Have older students write an appropriate fraction on each pizza slice.

Now explain to students that the restaurant puts eight (or sixteen) pieces of pepperoni on each pizza. Ask how many pieces would be on each slice of their pizzas if the pepperoni pieces were divided equally among the slices.

Mathematics

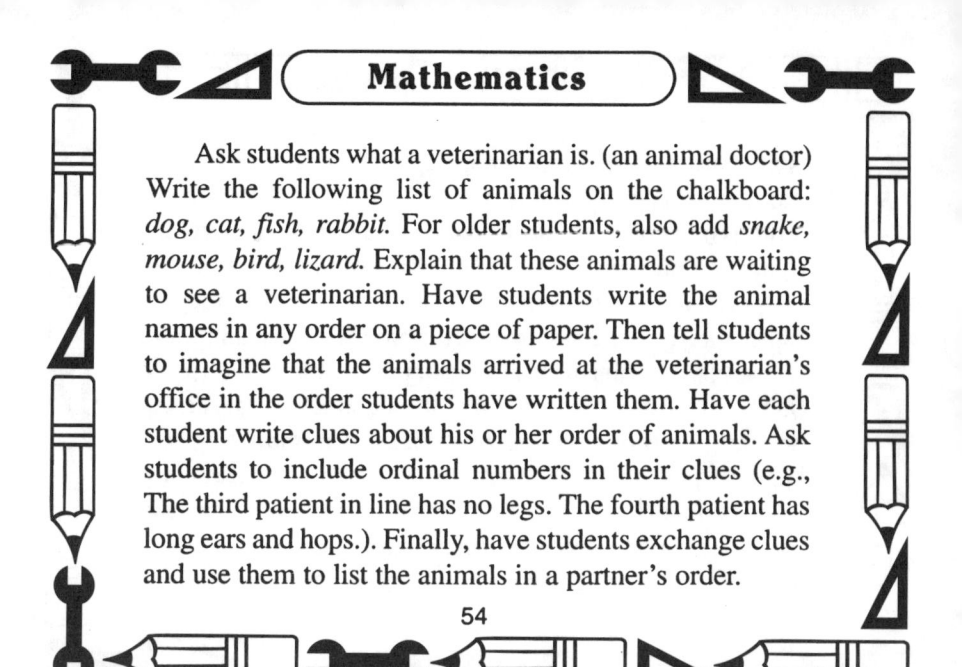

Ask students what a veterinarian is. (an animal doctor)
Write the following list of animals on the chalkboard:
dog, cat, fish, rabbit. For older students, also add *snake, mouse, bird, lizard.* Explain that these animals are waiting
to see a veterinarian. Have students write the animal
names in any order on a piece of paper. Then tell students
to imagine that the animals arrived at the veterinarian's
office in the order students have written them. Have each
student write clues about his or her order of animals. Ask
students to include ordinal numbers in their clues (e.g.,
The third patient in line has no legs. The fourth patient has
long ears and hops.). Finally, have students exchange clues
and use them to list the animals in a partner's order.

Mathematics

Ask students what bus drivers do. (drive people from place to place) Copy the following word problem onto the chalkboard: *A driver picks up four people, then picks up two more. At the next stop, two riders get off the bus and one gets on. Next, three riders get off and one gets on. How many riders are on the bus?*

Have younger students act out the problem to solve it. Have older students write number sentences. ($4 + 2 = 6 - 2 = 4 + 1 = 5 - 3 = 2 + 1 = 3$)

Allow students to write (act out) additional problems involving a bus and its riders.

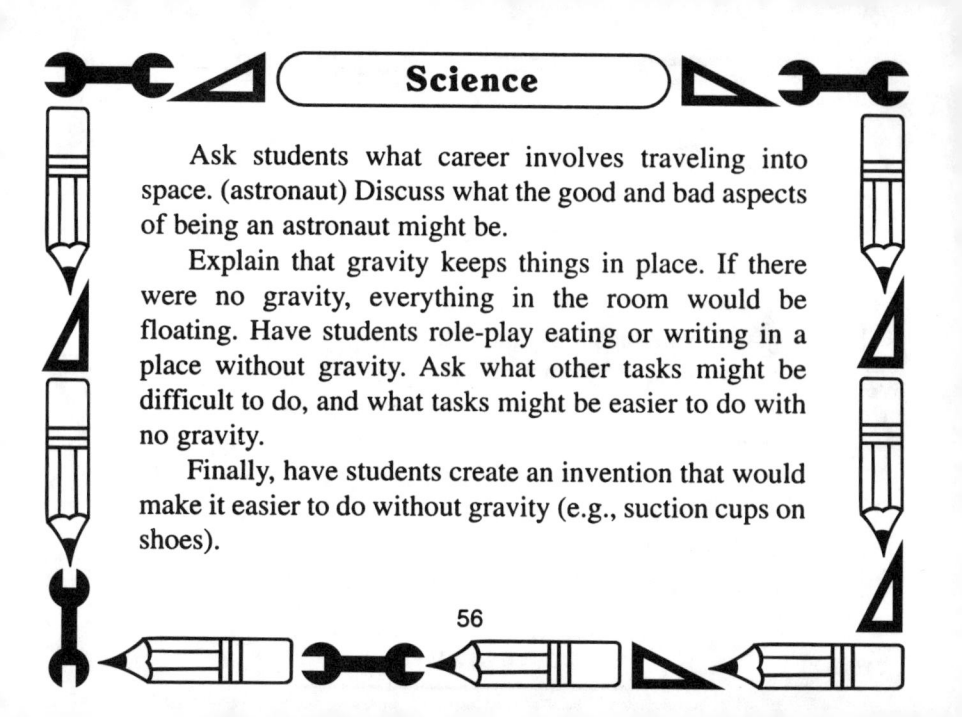

Science

Ask students what career involves traveling into space. (astronaut) Discuss what the good and bad aspects of being an astronaut might be.

Explain that gravity keeps things in place. If there were no gravity, everything in the room would be floating. Have students role-play eating or writing in a place without gravity. Ask what other tasks might be difficult to do, and what tasks might be easier to do with no gravity.

Finally, have students create an invention that would make it easier to do without gravity (e.g., suction cups on shoes).

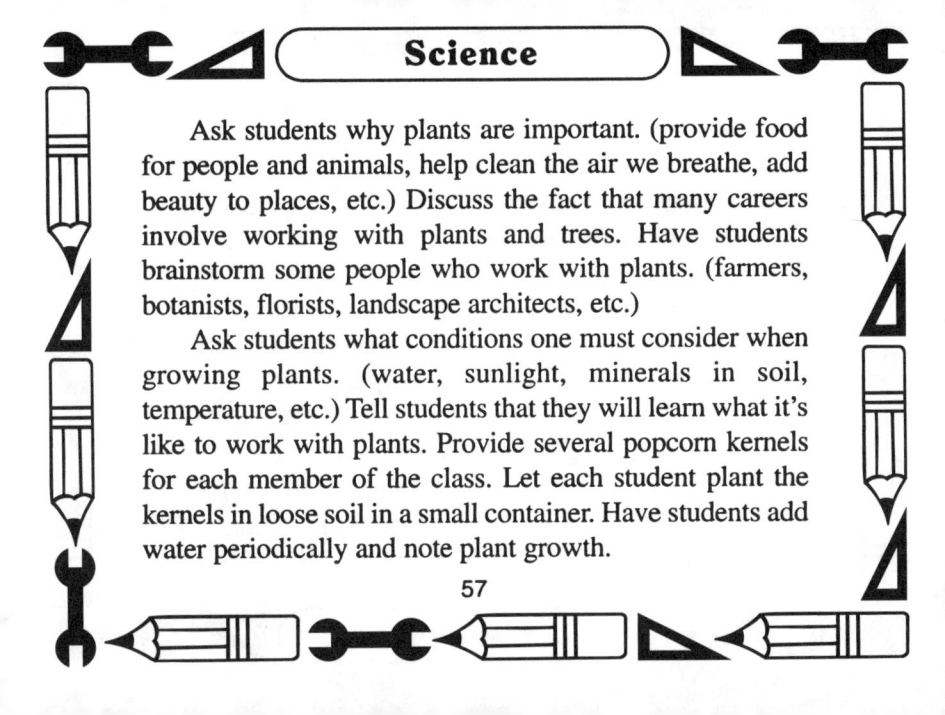

Science

Ask students why plants are important. (provide food for people and animals, help clean the air we breathe, add beauty to places, etc.) Discuss the fact that many careers involve working with plants and trees. Have students brainstorm some people who work with plants. (farmers, botanists, florists, landscape architects, etc.)

Ask students what conditions one must consider when growing plants. (water, sunlight, minerals in soil, temperature, etc.) Tell students that they will learn what it's like to work with plants. Provide several popcorn kernels for each member of the class. Let each student plant the kernels in loose soil in a small container. Have students add water periodically and note plant growth.

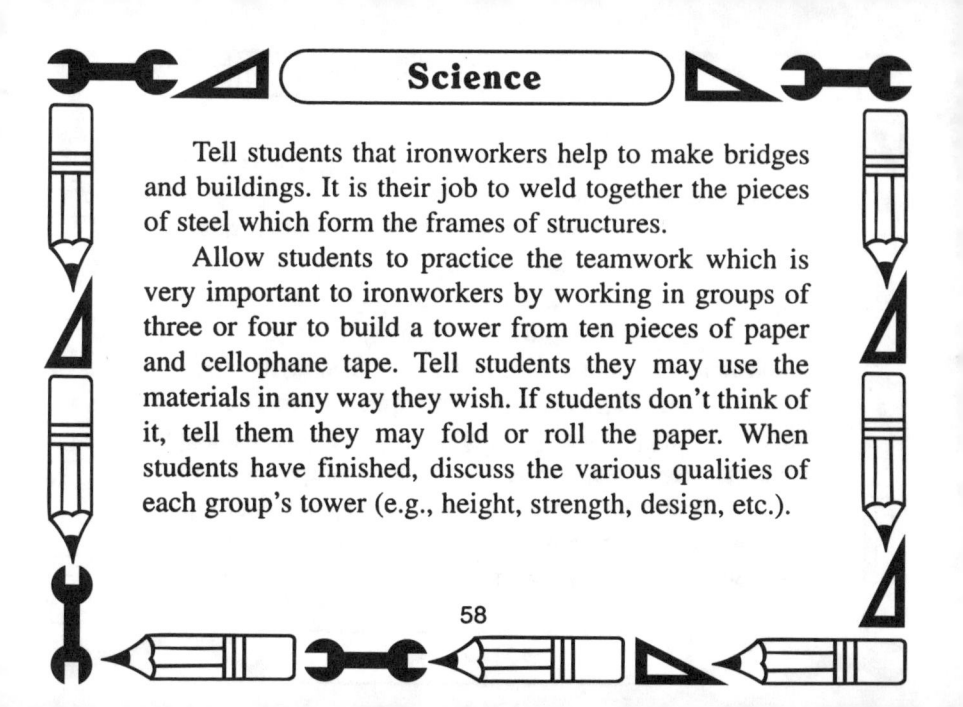

Science

Tell students that ironworkers help to make bridges and buildings. It is their job to weld together the pieces of steel which form the frames of structures.

Allow students to practice the teamwork which is very important to ironworkers by working in groups of three or four to build a tower from ten pieces of paper and cellophane tape. Tell students they may use the materials in any way they wish. If students don't think of it, tell them they may fold or roll the paper. When students have finished, discuss the various qualities of each group's tower (e.g., height, strength, design, etc.).

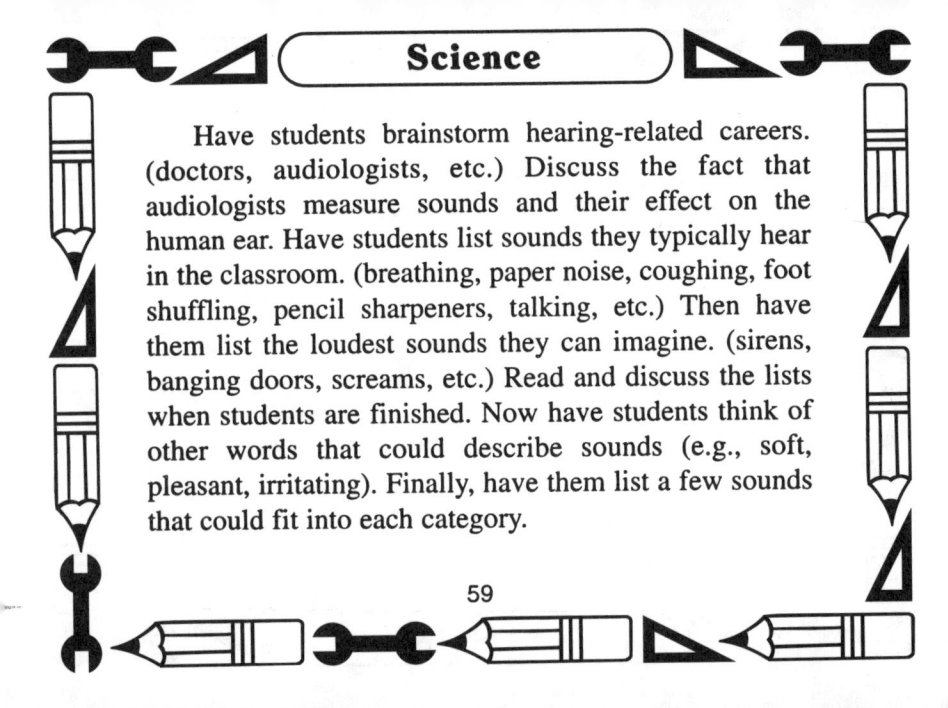

Science

Have students brainstorm hearing-related careers. (doctors, audiologists, etc.) Discuss the fact that audiologists measure sounds and their effect on the human ear. Have students list sounds they typically hear in the classroom. (breathing, paper noise, coughing, foot shuffling, pencil sharpeners, talking, etc.) Then have them list the loudest sounds they can imagine. (sirens, banging doors, screams, etc.) Read and discuss the lists when students are finished. Now have students think of other words that could describe sounds (e.g., soft, pleasant, irritating). Finally, have them list a few sounds that could fit into each category.

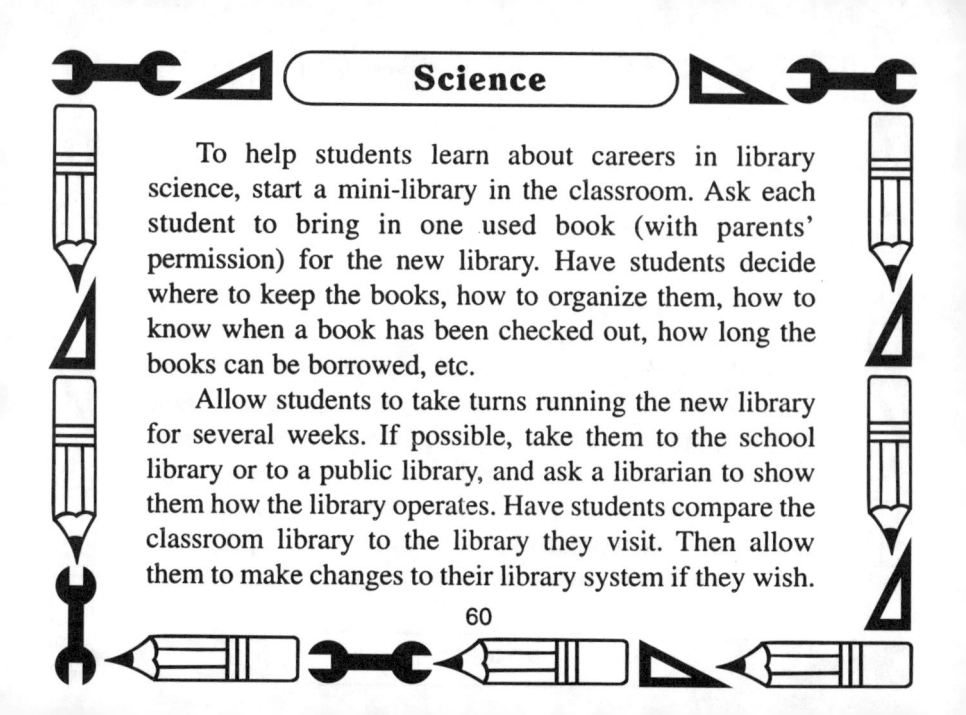

Science

To help students learn about careers in library science, start a mini-library in the classroom. Ask each student to bring in one used book (with parents' permission) for the new library. Have students decide where to keep the books, how to organize them, how to know when a book has been checked out, how long the books can be borrowed, etc.

Allow students to take turns running the new library for several weeks. If possible, take them to the school library or to a public library, and ask a librarian to show them how the library operates. Have students compare the classroom library to the library they visit. Then allow them to make changes to their library system if they wish.

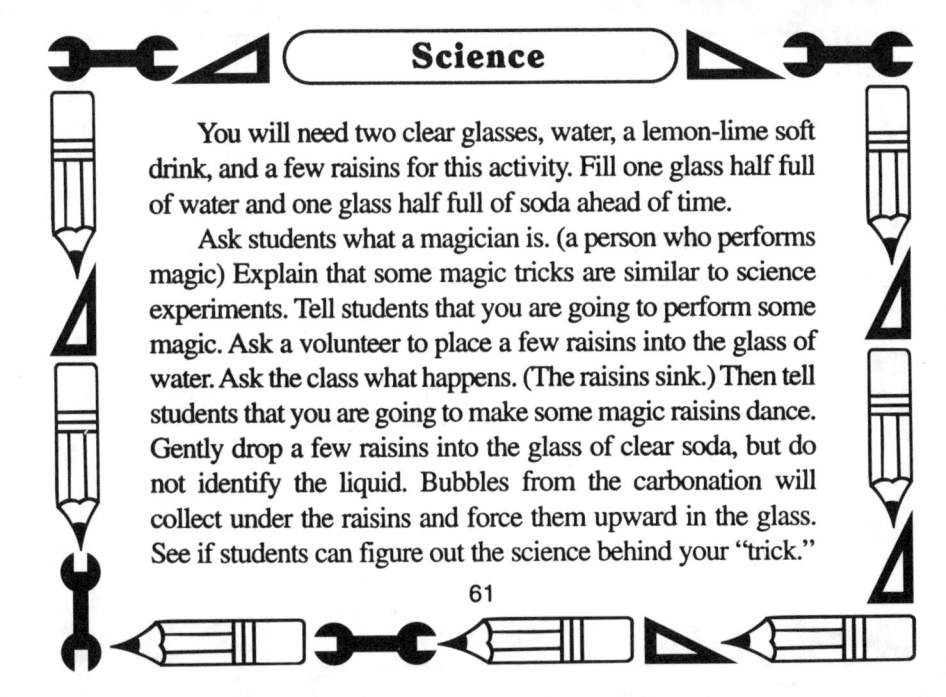

Science

You will need two clear glasses, water, a lemon-lime soft drink, and a few raisins for this activity. Fill one glass half full of water and one glass half full of soda ahead of time.

Ask students what a magician is. (a person who performs magic) Explain that some magic tricks are similar to science experiments. Tell students that you are going to perform some magic. Ask a volunteer to place a few raisins into the glass of water. Ask the class what happens. (The raisins sink.) Then tell students that you are going to make some magic raisins dance. Gently drop a few raisins into the glass of clear soda, but do not identify the liquid. Bubbles from the carbonation will collect under the raisins and force them upward in the glass. See if students can figure out the science behind your "trick."

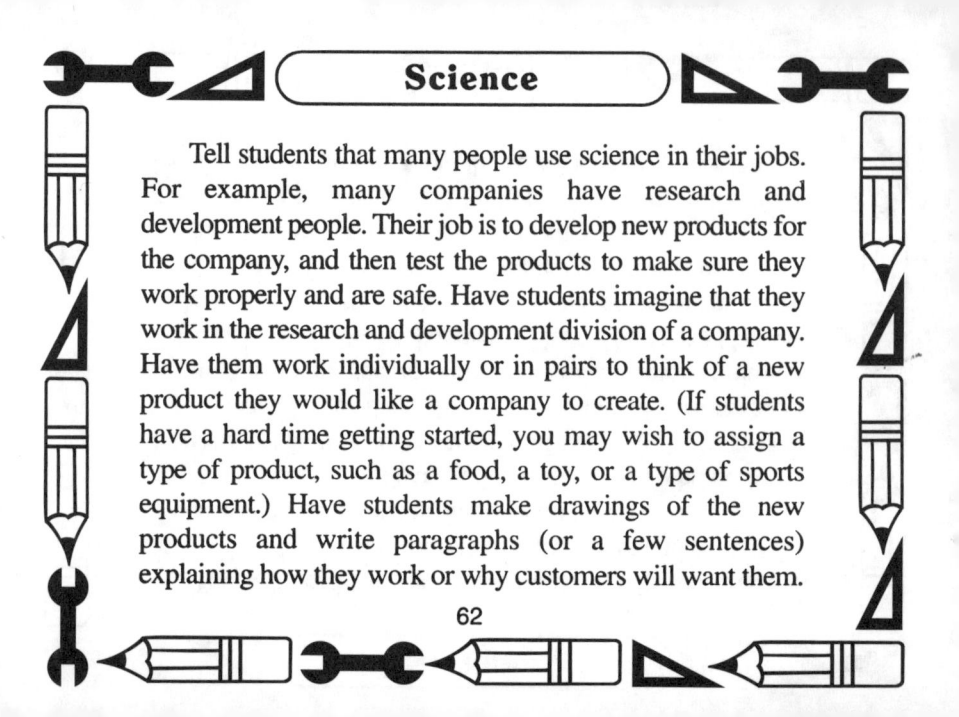

Science

Tell students that many people use science in their jobs. For example, many companies have research and development people. Their job is to develop new products for the company, and then test the products to make sure they work properly and are safe. Have students imagine that they work in the research and development division of a company. Have them work individually or in pairs to think of a new product they would like a company to create. (If students have a hard time getting started, you may wish to assign a type of product, such as a food, a toy, or a type of sports equipment.) Have students make drawings of the new products and write paragraphs (or a few sentences) explaining how they work or why customers will want them.

Science

Ask students if they have ever moved from one home to another. Explain that workers who help people to buy and sell homes are called real estate agents. Have students imagine that they are real estate agents. They are helping someone to sell a home, and they need to make the home as attractive as possible to people who may want to buy it. List the five senses on the chalkboard. Have students suggest ways to make the home appeal to each of the senses (e.g., make sure it looks clean, play soothing music, bake bread to make the house smell homey, offer a tasty snack to visitors, make sure the house is not too hot or too cold, etc.).

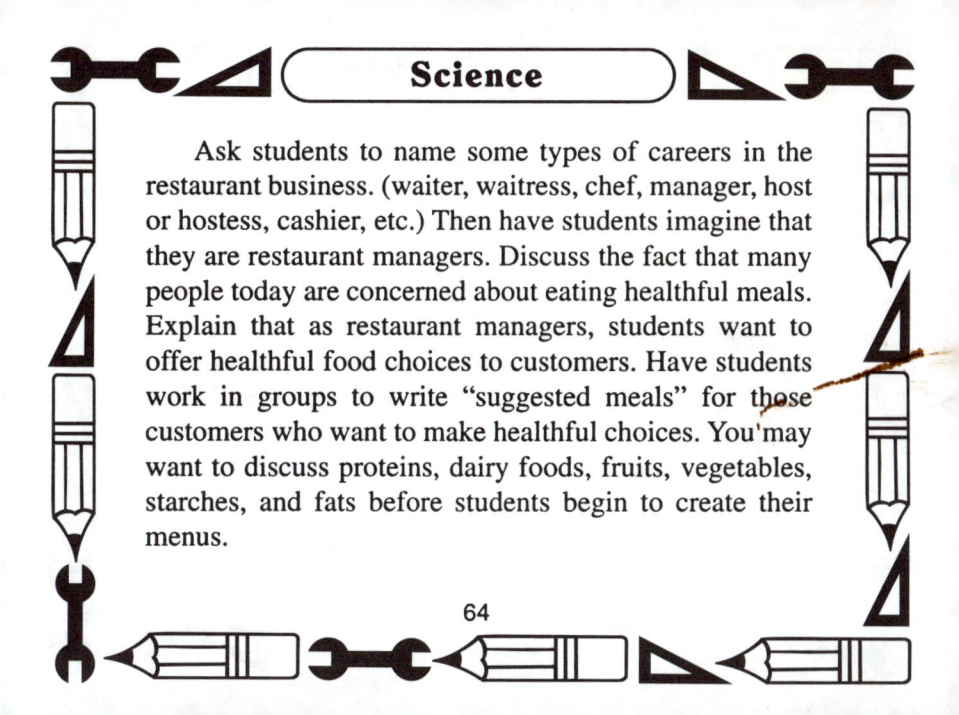

Science

Ask students to name some types of careers in the restaurant business. (waiter, waitress, chef, manager, host or hostess, cashier, etc.) Then have students imagine that they are restaurant managers. Discuss the fact that many people today are concerned about eating healthful meals. Explain that as restaurant managers, students want to offer healthful food choices to customers. Have students work in groups to write "suggested meals" for those customers who want to make healthful choices. You may want to discuss proteins, dairy foods, fruits, vegetables, starches, and fats before students begin to create their menus.

Science

You will need glass jars, rulers, and permanent markers for this activity. Ask students what kinds of businesses might be affected by rainfall. (construction, landscaping, etc.) Discuss the fact that sales for these businesses can be harmed if too much rain falls. Then have students work in pairs to create simple rain gauges. First, instruct each pair to place a ruler inside a jar and draw lines 1" apart on the outside of the jar, beginning at the bottom. Next, have students place their gauges outside where the jars will catch the rain. After the next rainfall, have students check the rain gauges to see how much rain fell.

Science

Ask students if they know what geologists do. (study rocks, caves, mountains, etc.) Allow your students to be geologists for a day. Have each student bring in a small rock, or take the class on a walk so students can find rocks. Then have each student carefully study his or her rock, taking note of its distinguishing traits. Older students can write detailed descriptions of the rocks. Have students form groups, mix up their rocks, then place the rocks in a row. Younger students can take turns identifying their rocks. Older students can exchange descriptions and try to find one another's rocks based on the written details.

As a follow-up activity, have students help you categorize all the rocks by shape, size, color, texture, etc.

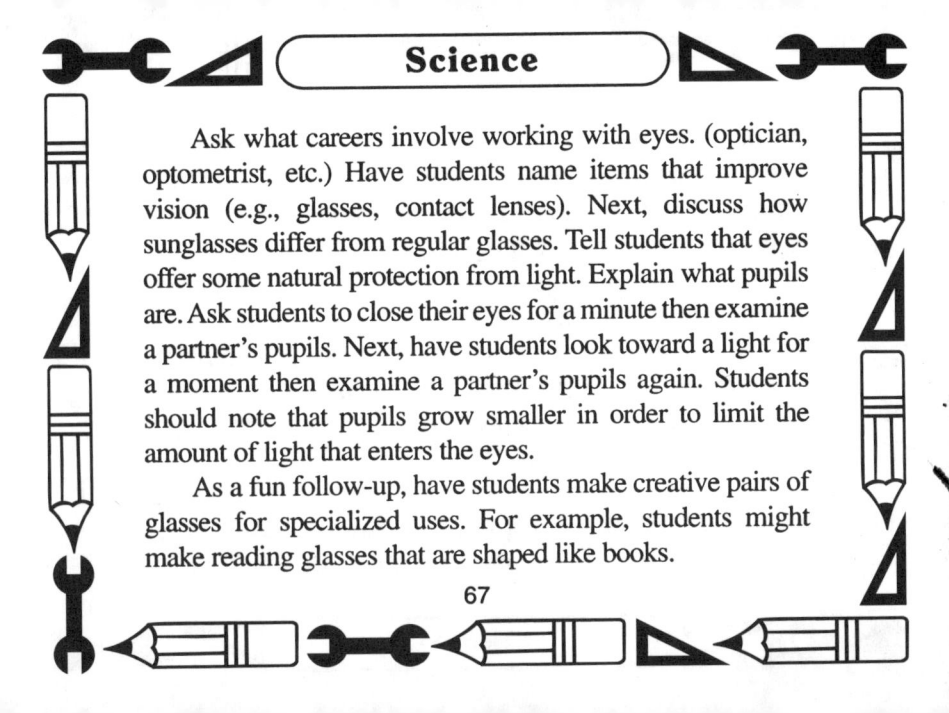

Science

Ask what careers involve working with eyes. (optician, optometrist, etc.) Have students name items that improve vision (e.g., glasses, contact lenses). Next, discuss how sunglasses differ from regular glasses. Tell students that eyes offer some natural protection from light. Explain what pupils are. Ask students to close their eyes for a minute then examine a partner's pupils. Next, have students look toward a light for a moment then examine a partner's pupils again. Students should note that pupils grow smaller in order to limit the amount of light that enters the eyes.

As a fun follow-up, have students make creative pairs of glasses for specialized uses. For example, students might make reading glasses that are shaped like books.

Science

Explain to students that there are many law enforcement careers. Ask what law enforcement positions they can think of (e.g., police officers, FBI agents, detectives). Tell students that markings on their hands, called fingerprints, leave tracks on many items they handle. Discuss the fact that natural oils and ridges on students' fingertips leave invisible marks. Help students use an ink pad to show their fingerprints on paper. Allow students to form groups and talk about how their fingerprints are alike and different. When working with older students, you may wish to have each student make two copies of a fingerprint, then mix up one set of a group's fingerprints and have students compare the prints to the second set to match them.

Science

You will need a blown-up balloon, combs, wool cloth, and bits of paper for this activity. Ask students when they use electricity, then have them think of careers that involve working with electricity. (electricians, electrical engineers, etc.) Discuss the fact that you can create a kind of electricity (static electricity) that will hold a balloon against the classroom wall. First, hold a ballon against the wall to show that it will not stick. Next, rub the side of the balloon against your hair several times, then place the balloon against the wall. The balloon will stick to the wall.

Have small groups of students create additional static electricity by firmly rubbing a wool cloth on a comb. The comb will then pick up small bits of paper.

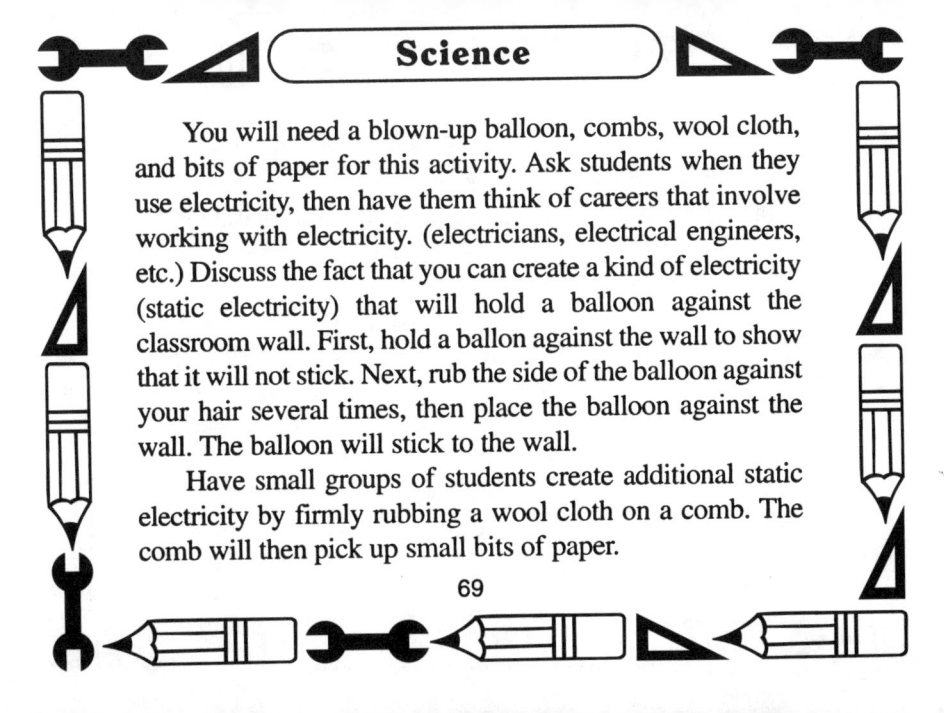

Science

Ask students what a dentist is. (a doctor who takes care of teeth) Discuss ways people can make sure their teeth and gums stay healthy (e.g., brushing, flossing, eating properly, having dental checkups regularly). Explain that people grow two sets of teeth. Baby teeth begin to fall out when children are about five years old to make room for permanent teeth. Adults have 32 permanent teeth. Allow students to share their experiences with "wiggly" and lost teeth.

Have small groups of students create posters that depict good dental care. The posters could contain pictures of children caring for their teeth, pictures of children visiting the dentist, and/or lists of ways to care for teeth. Allow time for students to show the posters to other groups.

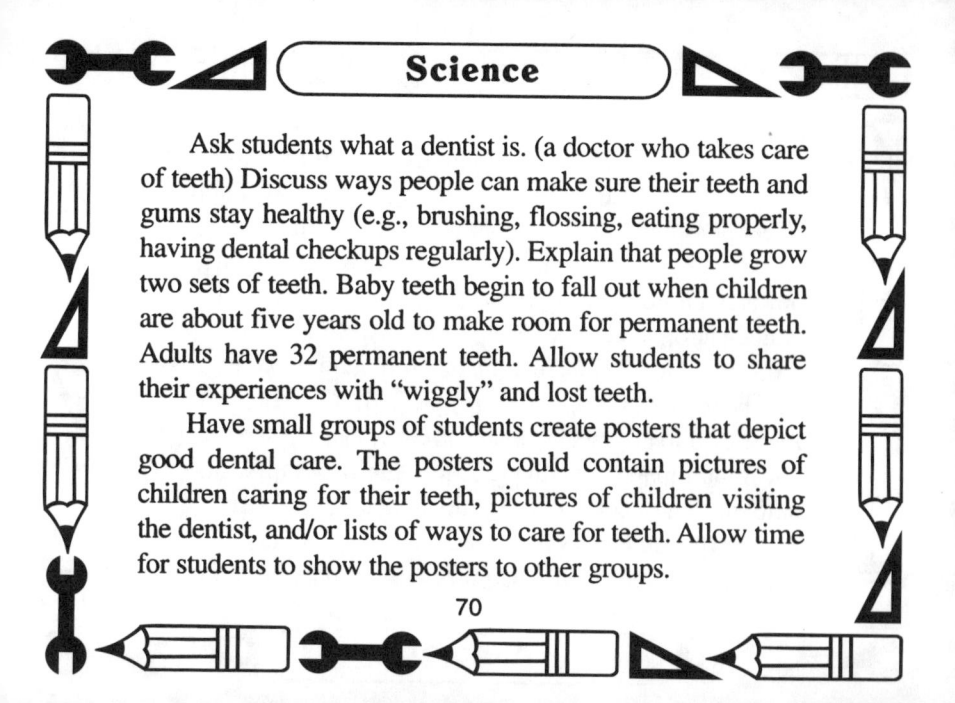

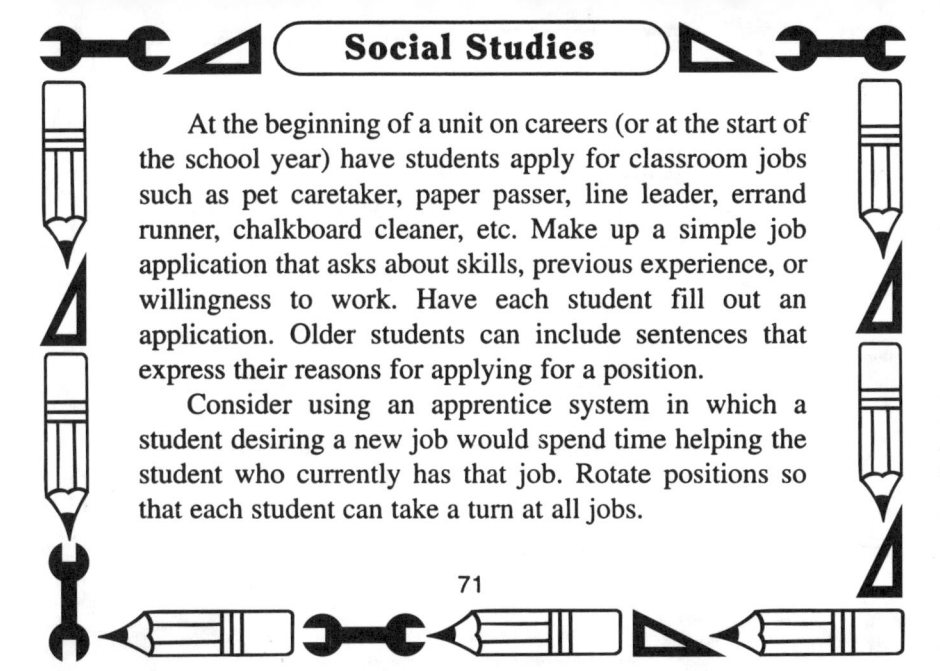

Social Studies

At the beginning of a unit on careers (or at the start of the school year) have students apply for classroom jobs such as pet caretaker, paper passer, line leader, errand runner, chalkboard cleaner, etc. Make up a simple job application that asks about skills, previous experience, or willingness to work. Have each student fill out an application. Older students can include sentences that express their reasons for applying for a position.

Consider using an apprentice system in which a student desiring a new job would spend time helping the student who currently has that job. Rotate positions so that each student can take a turn at all jobs.

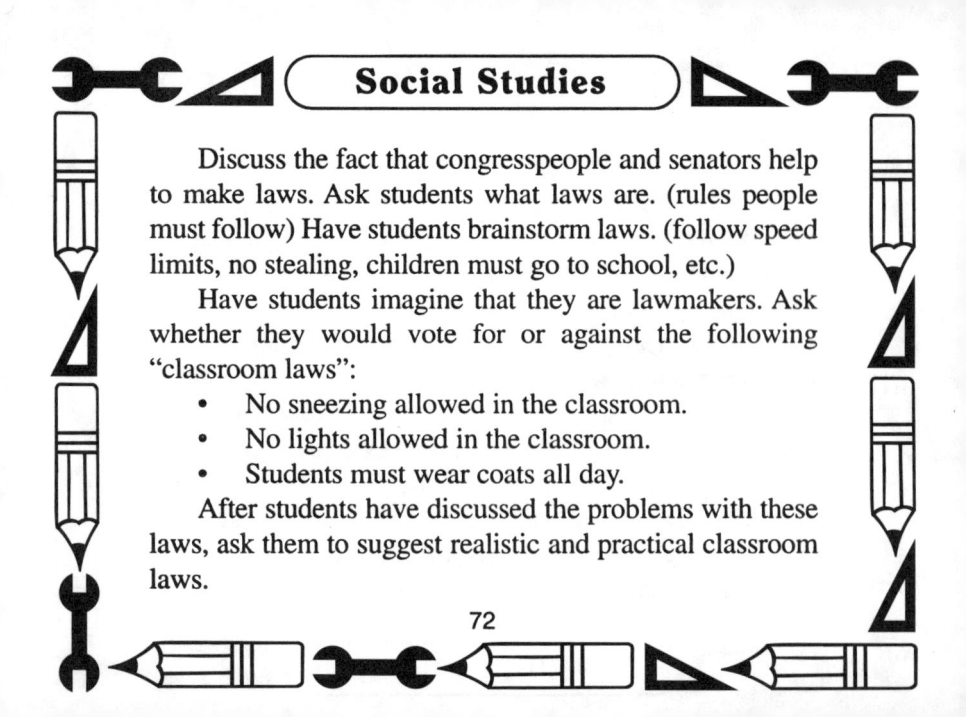

Social Studies

Discuss the fact that congresspeople and senators help to make laws. Ask students what laws are. (rules people must follow) Have students brainstorm laws. (follow speed limits, no stealing, children must go to school, etc.)

Have students imagine that they are lawmakers. Ask whether they would vote for or against the following "classroom laws":

- No sneezing allowed in the classroom.
- No lights allowed in the classroom.
- Students must wear coats all day.

After students have discussed the problems with these laws, ask them to suggest realistic and practical classroom laws.

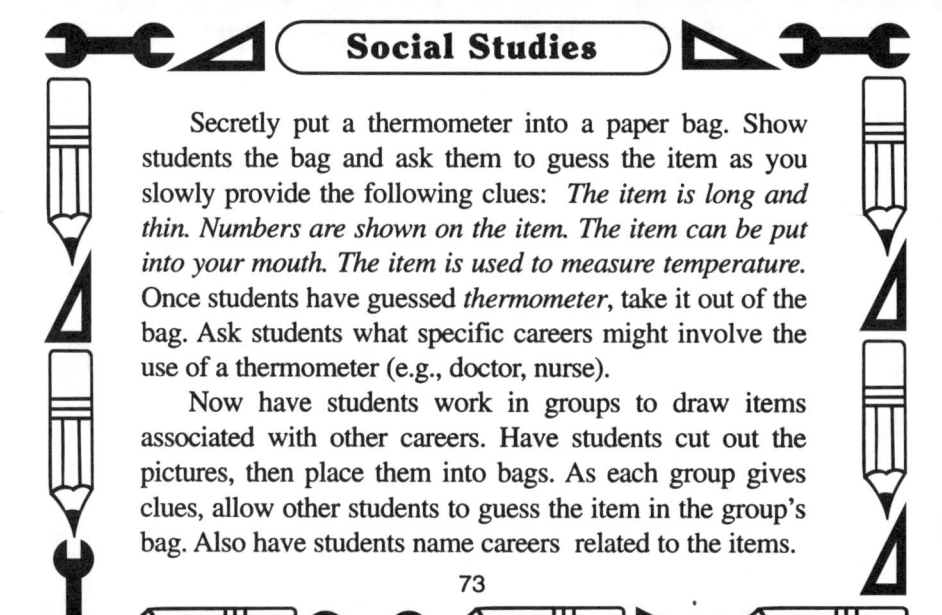

Social Studies

Secretly put a thermometer into a paper bag. Show students the bag and ask them to guess the item as you slowly provide the following clues: *The item is long and thin. Numbers are shown on the item. The item can be put into your mouth. The item is used to measure temperature.* Once students have guessed *thermometer*, take it out of the bag. Ask students what specific careers might involve the use of a thermometer (e.g., doctor, nurse).

Now have students work in groups to draw items associated with other careers. Have students cut out the pictures, then place them into bags. As each group gives clues, allow other students to guess the item in the group's bag. Also have students name careers related to the items.

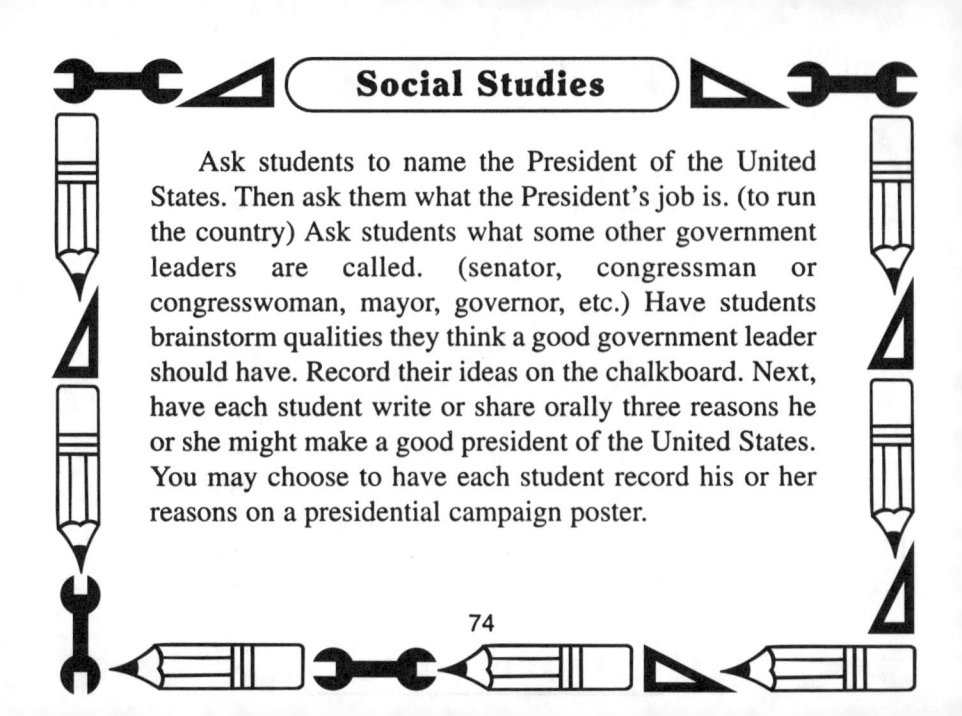

Social Studies

Ask students to name the President of the United States. Then ask them what the President's job is. (to run the country) Ask students what some other government leaders are called. (senator, congressman or congresswoman, mayor, governor, etc.) Have students brainstorm qualities they think a good government leader should have. Record their ideas on the chalkboard. Next, have each student write or share orally three reasons he or she might make a good president of the United States. You may choose to have each student record his or her reasons on a presidential campaign poster.

Social Studies

Ask students if they know what travel agents do. Explain that travel agents help people plan trips. They make hotel and flight reservations, provide information about things to do on vacations, etc. Discuss what kinds of questions a travel agent might ask a client before planning a trip. (when, where, how long, method of transportation, interests, reason for trip, etc.) Tell students that they are going to act as travel agents. Have students work in pairs to plan simple trips. Each pair should decide where to go and how to get there. Older students can also write simple itineraries that include each day's activities. Have students use maps to determine possible travel routes and means of transportation.

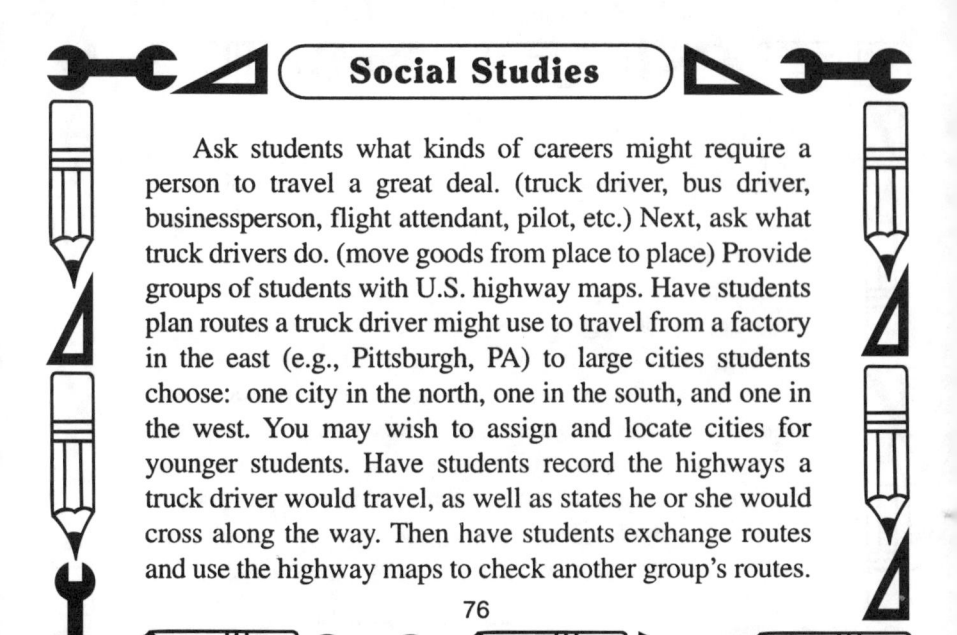

Social Studies

Ask students what kinds of careers might require a person to travel a great deal. (truck driver, bus driver, businessperson, flight attendant, pilot, etc.) Next, ask what truck drivers do. (move goods from place to place) Provide groups of students with U.S. highway maps. Have students plan routes a truck driver might use to travel from a factory in the east (e.g., Pittsburgh, PA) to large cities students choose: one city in the north, one in the south, and one in the west. You may wish to assign and locate cities for younger students. Have students record the highways a truck driver would travel, as well as states he or she would cross along the way. Then have students exchange routes and use the highway maps to check another group's routes.

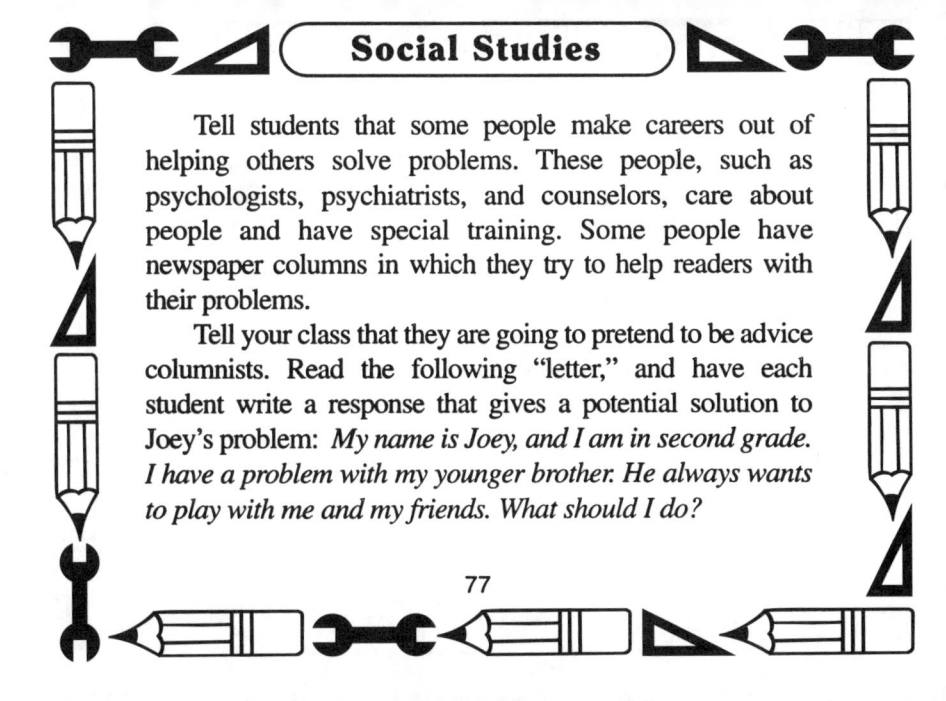

Social Studies

Tell students that some people make careers out of helping others solve problems. These people, such as psychologists, psychiatrists, and counselors, care about people and have special training. Some people have newspaper columns in which they try to help readers with their problems.

Tell your class that they are going to pretend to be advice columnists. Read the following "letter," and have each student write a response that gives a potential solution to Joey's problem: *My name is Joey, and I am in second grade. I have a problem with my younger brother. He always wants to play with me and my friends. What should I do?*

Social Studies

Ask students if they know what architects do. (design buildings that suit the people who will live or work in them) Ask students to imagine having a house made completely of glass. Have them list all the good things a glass house might offer (bright, allows one to see outside easily, great for star watching, etc.), and then all of the problems having glass walls, floors, and ceilings might cause (difficult to have privacy, hard to keep clean, can't put nails in walls, hot in summer and cold in winter, etc.).

Finally, have students work in groups to brainstorm another type of house that is very different from most homes today (e.g., one made of pillows). Have the groups draw the houses, then list (describe) their good points and bad points.

Social Studies

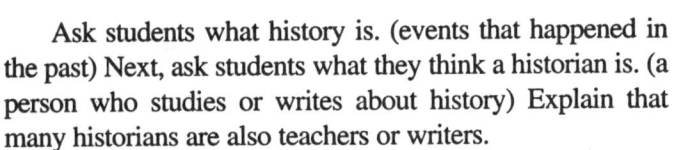

Ask students what history is. (events that happened in the past) Next, ask students what they think a historian is. (a person who studies or writes about history) Explain that many historians are also teachers or writers.

Tell students that they are going to have the opportunity to become historians by recording the history of the class. Begin by having students brainstorm major events that have happened during the year (e.g., field trips, classroom visitors, important current events, etc.). Then have students work in groups to record that history in any form they choose. Younger students may want to illustrate the events. Older students might create a timeline. Encourage students to present the information creatively.

Social Studies

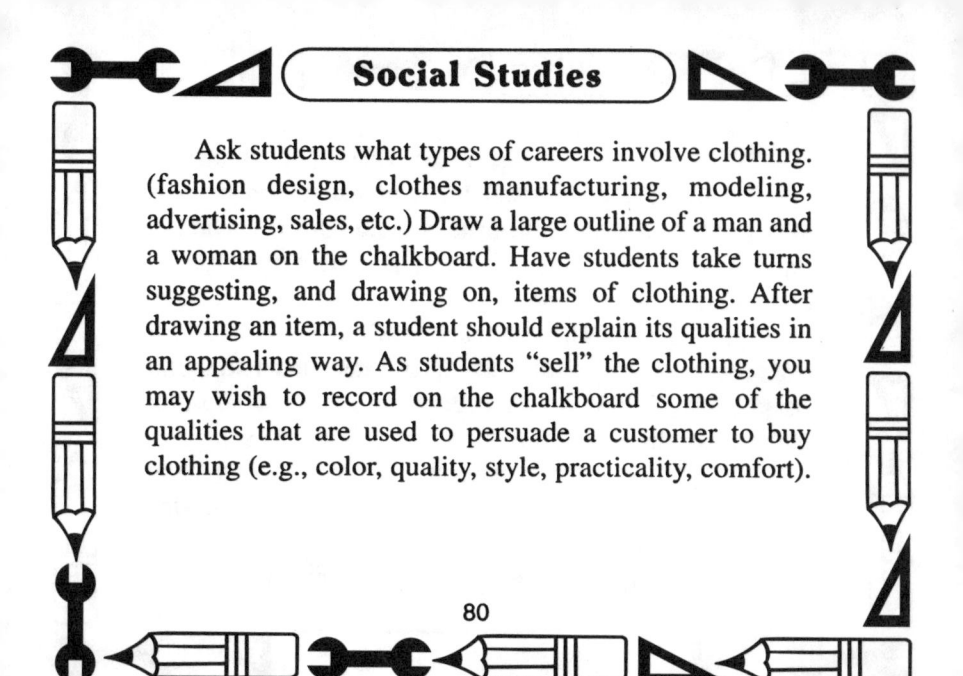

Ask students what types of careers involve clothing. (fashion design, clothes manufacturing, modeling, advertising, sales, etc.) Draw a large outline of a man and a woman on the chalkboard. Have students take turns suggesting, and drawing on, items of clothing. After drawing an item, a student should explain its qualities in an appealing way. As students "sell" the clothing, you may wish to record on the chalkboard some of the qualities that are used to persuade a customer to buy clothing (e.g., color, quality, style, practicality, comfort).

Social Studies

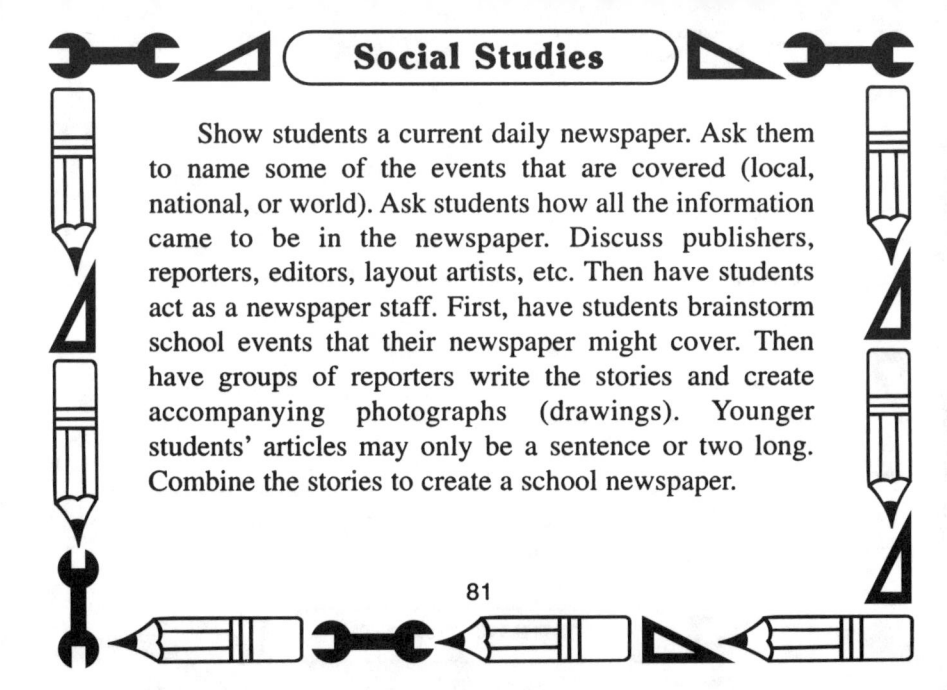

Show students a current daily newspaper. Ask them to name some of the events that are covered (local, national, or world). Ask students how all the information came to be in the newspaper. Discuss publishers, reporters, editors, layout artists, etc. Then have students act as a newspaper staff. First, have students brainstorm school events that their newspaper might cover. Then have groups of reporters write the stories and create accompanying photographs (drawings). Younger students' articles may only be a sentence or two long. Combine the stories to create a school newspaper.

Social Studies

Ask students what the environment is. (the world around them) Discuss the fact that many people have careers that involve protecting or improving the environment. Ask students to list people who help the environment. (park rangers, forest fire fighters, water treatment workers, scientists who find solutions to pollution, etc.)

Tell students that the three main areas of the environment are air, water, and land. Next, have students work in groups to think of at least one way they can protect or improve each area of the environment. Have students record their ideas with words and/or pictures. Ask them to share their ideas with the rest of the class.

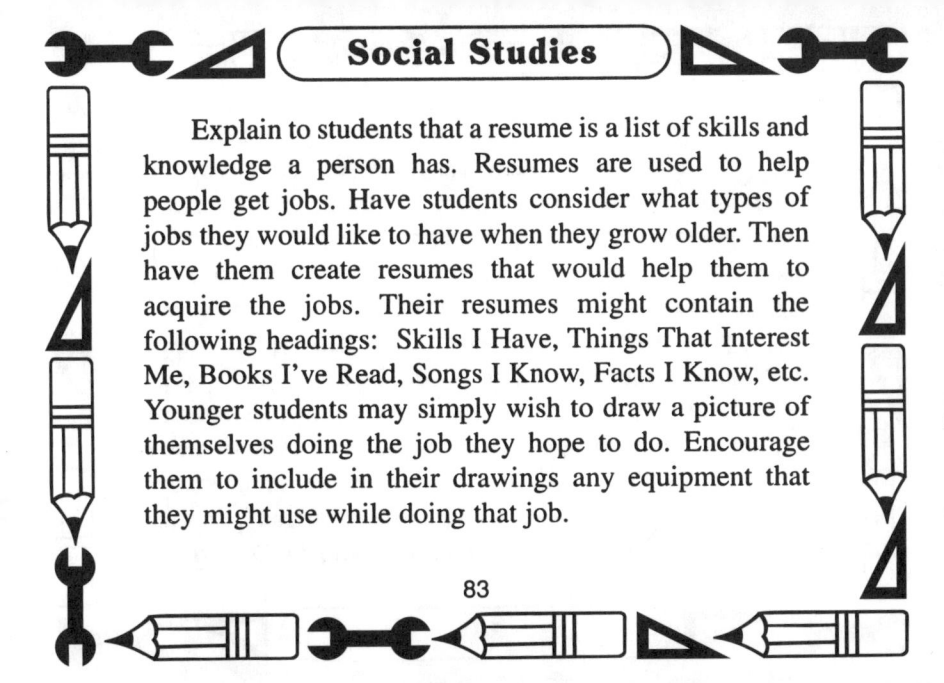

Social Studies

Explain to students that a resume is a list of skills and knowledge a person has. Resumes are used to help people get jobs. Have students consider what types of jobs they would like to have when they grow older. Then have them create resumes that would help them to acquire the jobs. Their resumes might contain the following headings: Skills I Have, Things That Interest Me, Books I've Read, Songs I Know, Facts I Know, etc. Younger students may simply wish to draw a picture of themselves doing the job they hope to do. Encourage them to include in their drawings any equipment that they might use while doing that job.

Art

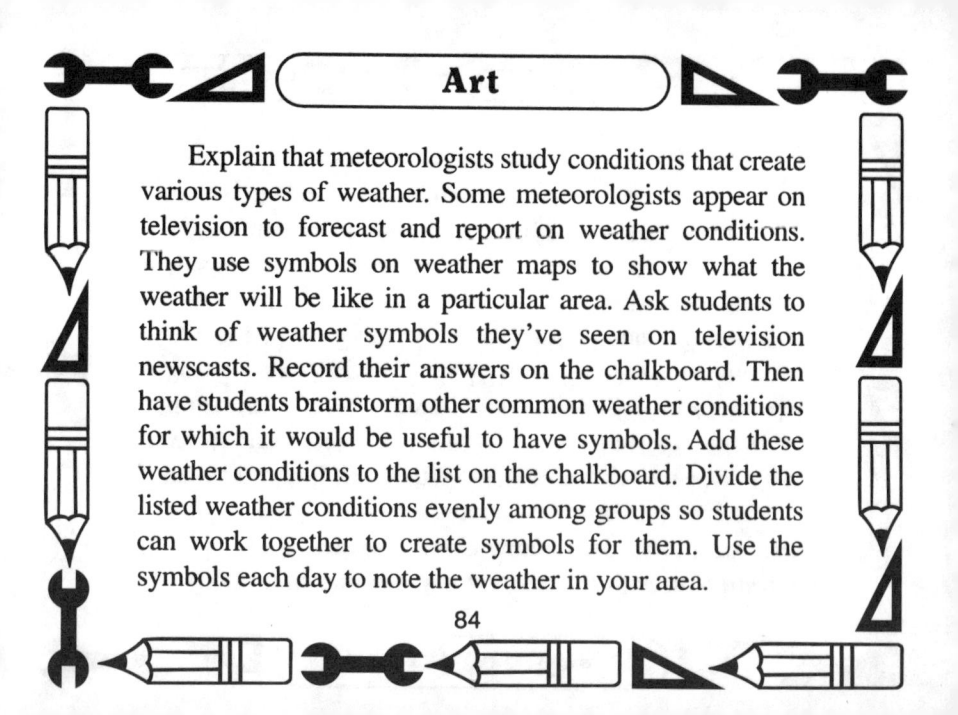

Explain that meteorologists study conditions that create various types of weather. Some meteorologists appear on television to forecast and report on weather conditions. They use symbols on weather maps to show what the weather will be like in a particular area. Ask students to think of weather symbols they've seen on television newscasts. Record their answers on the chalkboard. Then have students brainstorm other common weather conditions for which it would be useful to have symbols. Add these weather conditions to the list on the chalkboard. Divide the listed weather conditions evenly among groups so students can work together to create symbols for them. Use the symbols each day to note the weather in your area.

Art

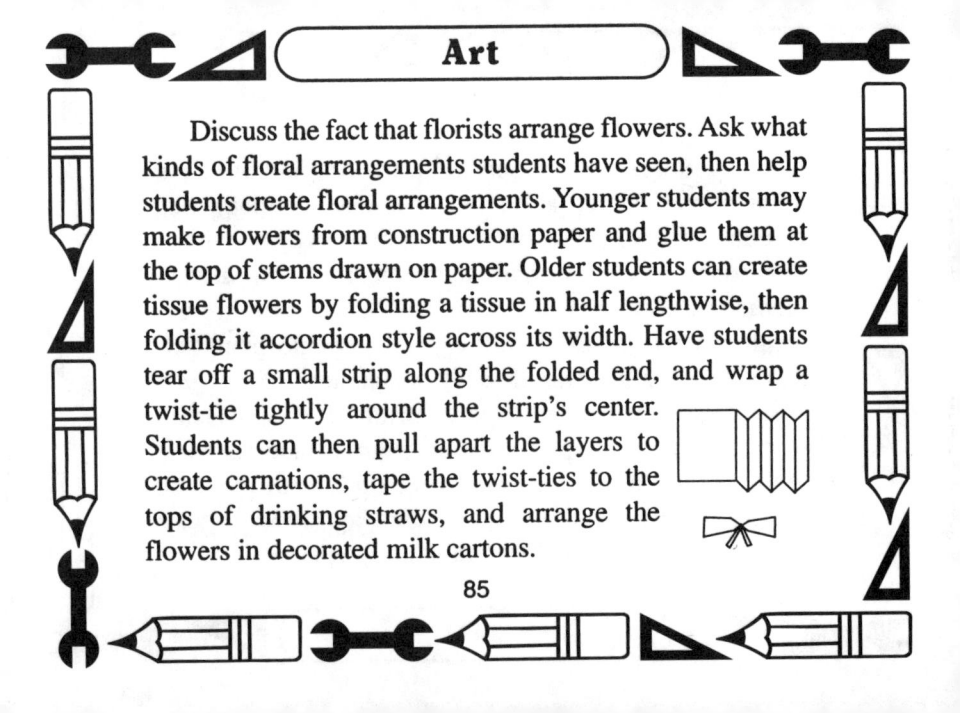

Discuss the fact that florists arrange flowers. Ask what kinds of floral arrangements students have seen, then help students create floral arrangements. Younger students may make flowers from construction paper and glue them at the top of stems drawn on paper. Older students can create tissue flowers by folding a tissue in half lengthwise, then folding it accordion style across its width. Have students tear off a small strip along the folded end, and wrap a twist-tie tightly around the strip's center. Students can then pull apart the layers to create carnations, tape the twist-ties to the tops of drinking straws, and arrange the flowers in decorated milk cartons.

Art

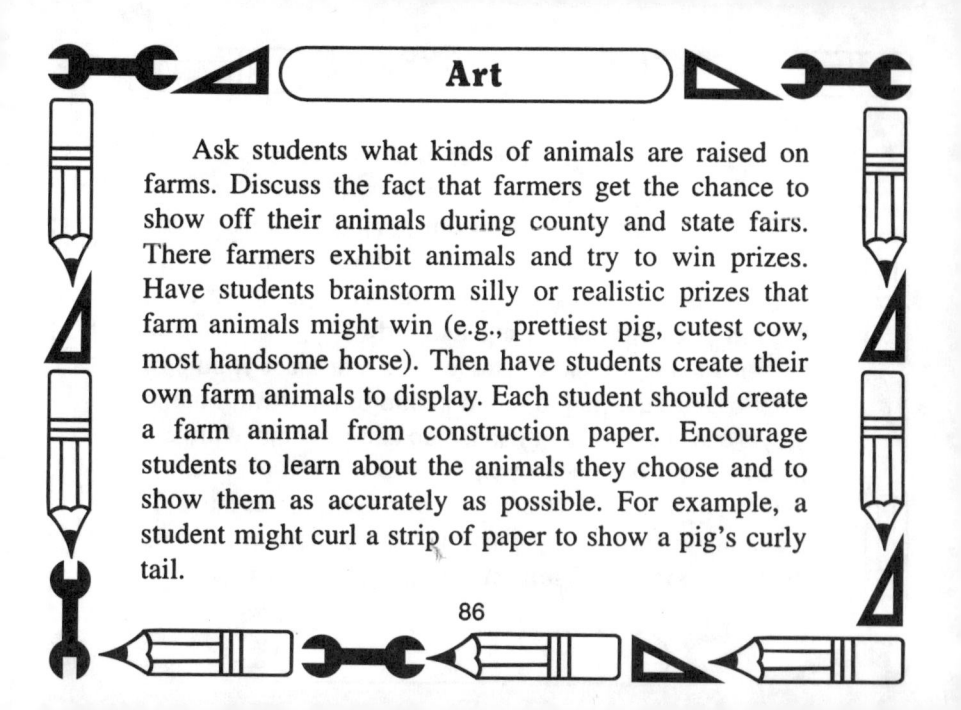

Ask students what kinds of animals are raised on farms. Discuss the fact that farmers get the chance to show off their animals during county and state fairs. There farmers exhibit animals and try to win prizes. Have students brainstorm silly or realistic prizes that farm animals might win (e.g., prettiest pig, cutest cow, most handsome horse). Then have students create their own farm animals to display. Each student should create a farm animal from construction paper. Encourage students to learn about the animals they choose and to show them as accurately as possible. For example, a student might curl a strip of paper to show a pig's curly tail.

Art

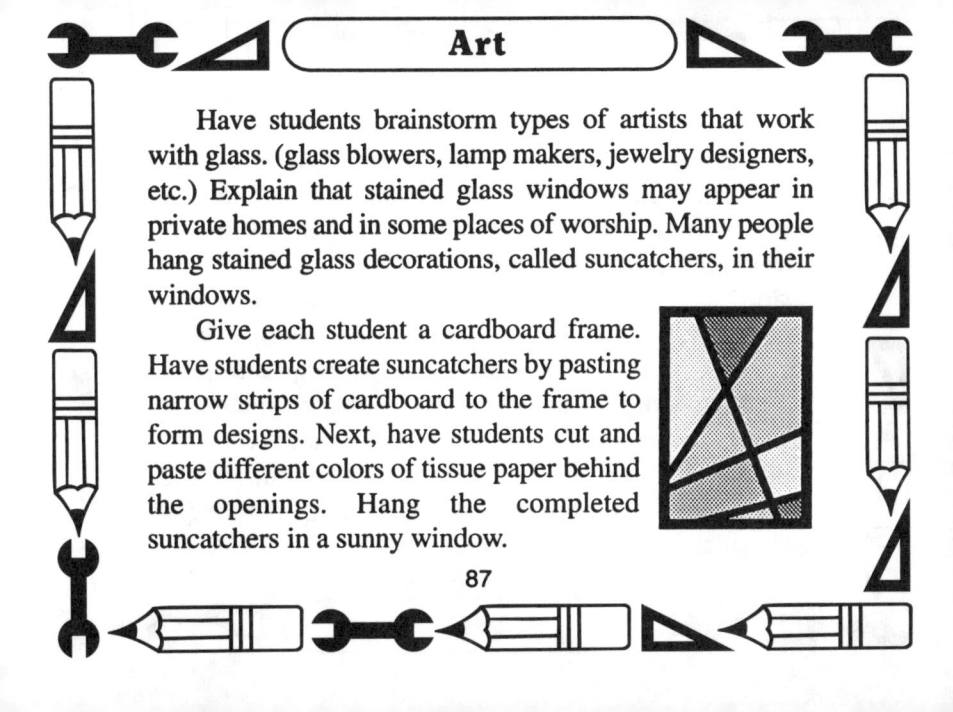

Have students brainstorm types of artists that work with glass. (glass blowers, lamp makers, jewelry designers, etc.) Explain that stained glass windows may appear in private homes and in some places of worship. Many people hang stained glass decorations, called suncatchers, in their windows.

Give each student a cardboard frame. Have students create suncatchers by pasting narrow strips of cardboard to the frame to form designs. Next, have students cut and paste different colors of tissue paper behind the openings. Hang the completed suncatchers in a sunny window.

Art

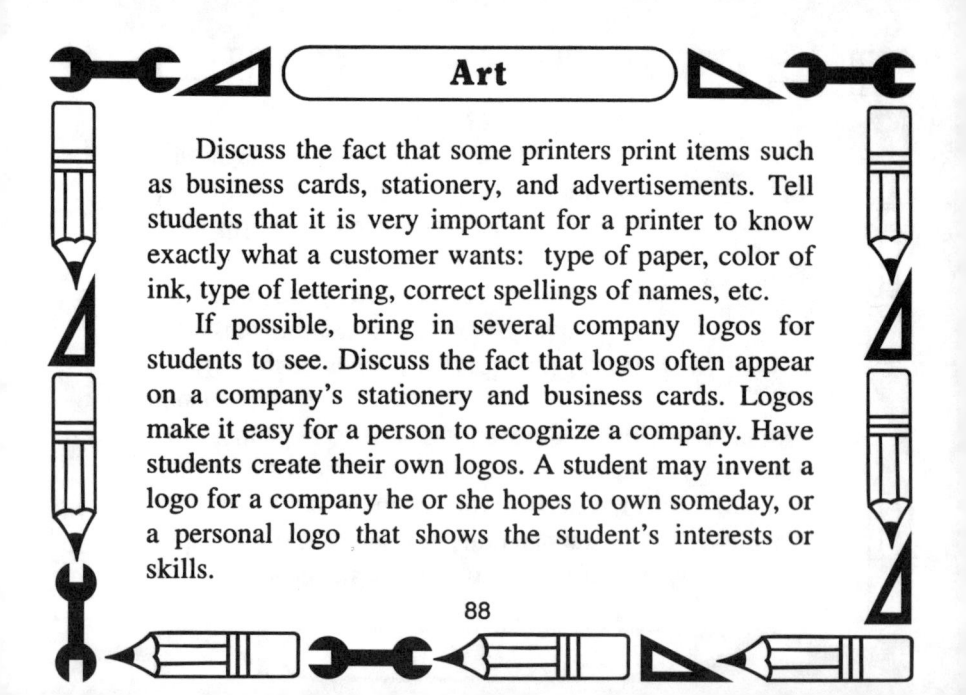

Discuss the fact that some printers print items such as business cards, stationery, and advertisements. Tell students that it is very important for a printer to know exactly what a customer wants: type of paper, color of ink, type of lettering, correct spellings of names, etc.

If possible, bring in several company logos for students to see. Discuss the fact that logos often appear on a company's stationery and business cards. Logos make it easy for a person to recognize a company. Have students create their own logos. A student may invent a logo for a company he or she hopes to own someday, or a personal logo that shows the student's interests or skills.

Art

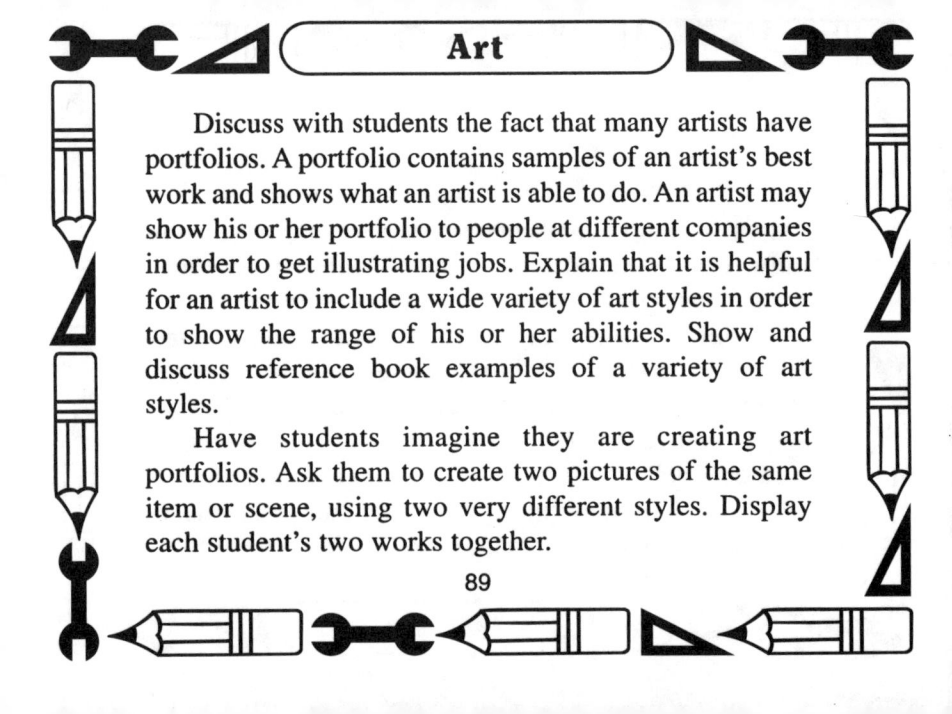

Discuss with students the fact that many artists have portfolios. A portfolio contains samples of an artist's best work and shows what an artist is able to do. An artist may show his or her portfolio to people at different companies in order to get illustrating jobs. Explain that it is helpful for an artist to include a wide variety of art styles in order to show the range of his or her abilities. Show and discuss reference book examples of a variety of art styles.

Have students imagine they are creating art portfolios. Ask them to create two pictures of the same item or scene, using two very different styles. Display each student's two works together.

Art

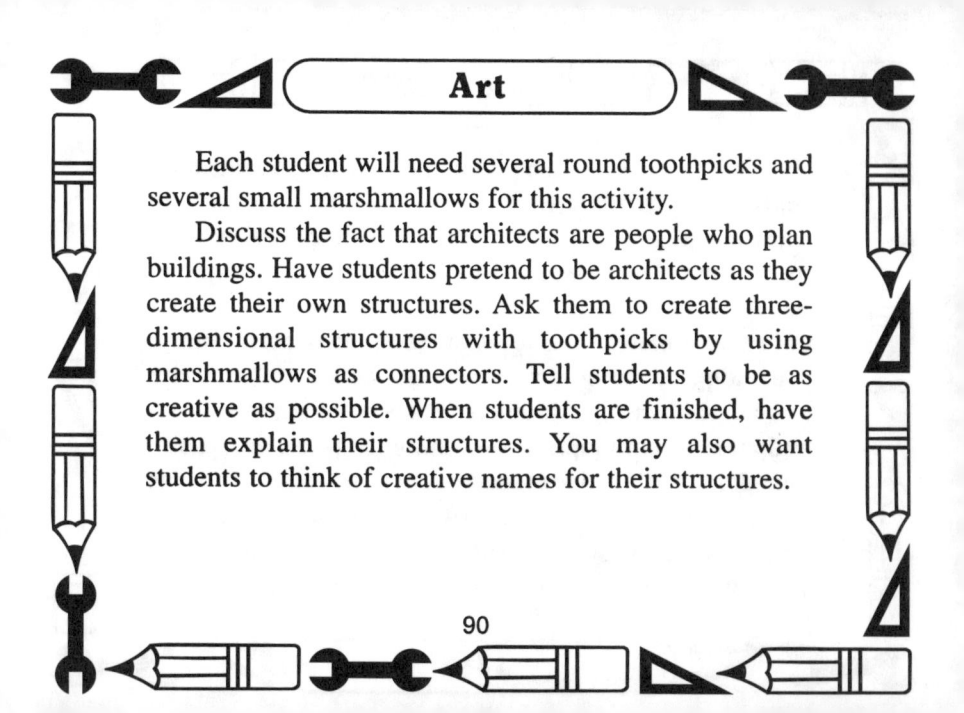

Each student will need several round toothpicks and several small marshmallows for this activity.

Discuss the fact that architects are people who plan buildings. Have students pretend to be architects as they create their own structures. Ask them to create three-dimensional structures with toothpicks by using marshmallows as connectors. Tell students to be as creative as possible. When students are finished, have them explain their structures. You may also want students to think of creative names for their structures.

Art

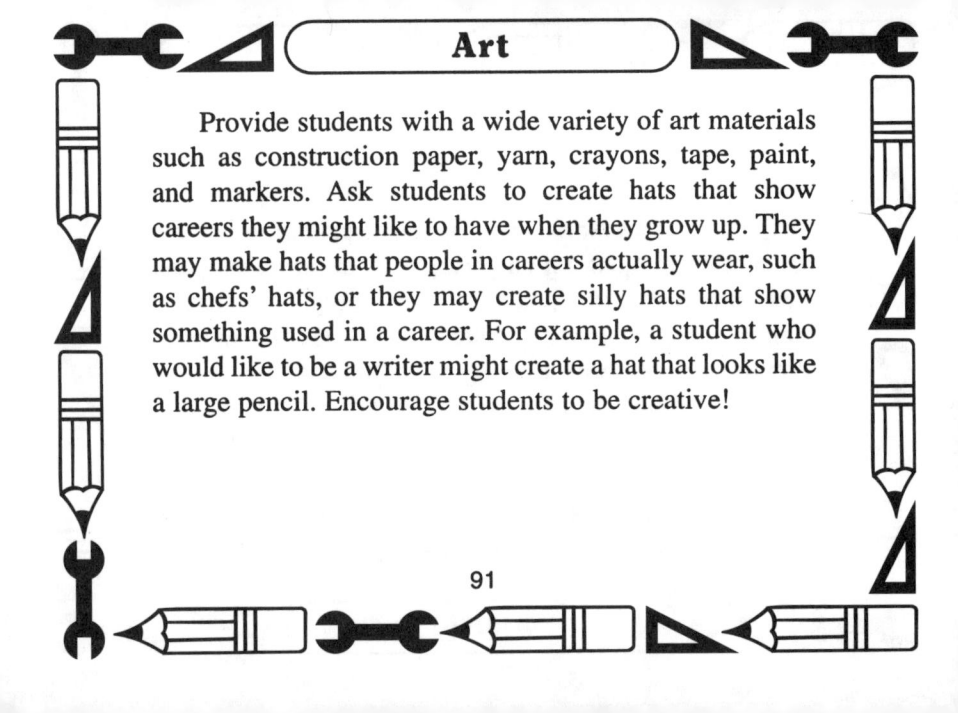

Provide students with a wide variety of art materials such as construction paper, yarn, crayons, tape, paint, and markers. Ask students to create hats that show careers they might like to have when they grow up. They may make hats that people in careers actually wear, such as chefs' hats, or they may create silly hats that show something used in a career. For example, a student who would like to be a writer might create a hat that looks like a large pencil. Encourage students to be creative!

Music

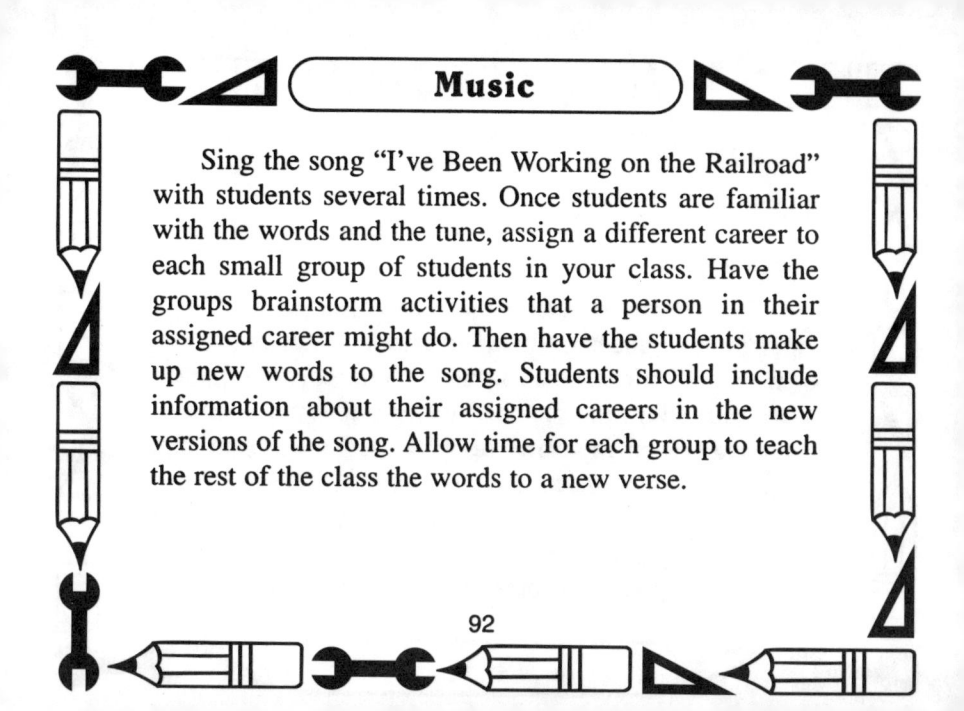

Sing the song "I've Been Working on the Railroad" with students several times. Once students are familiar with the words and the tune, assign a different career to each small group of students in your class. Have the groups brainstorm activities that a person in their assigned career might do. Then have the students make up new words to the song. Students should include information about their assigned careers in the new versions of the song. Allow time for each group to teach the rest of the class the words to a new verse.

Music

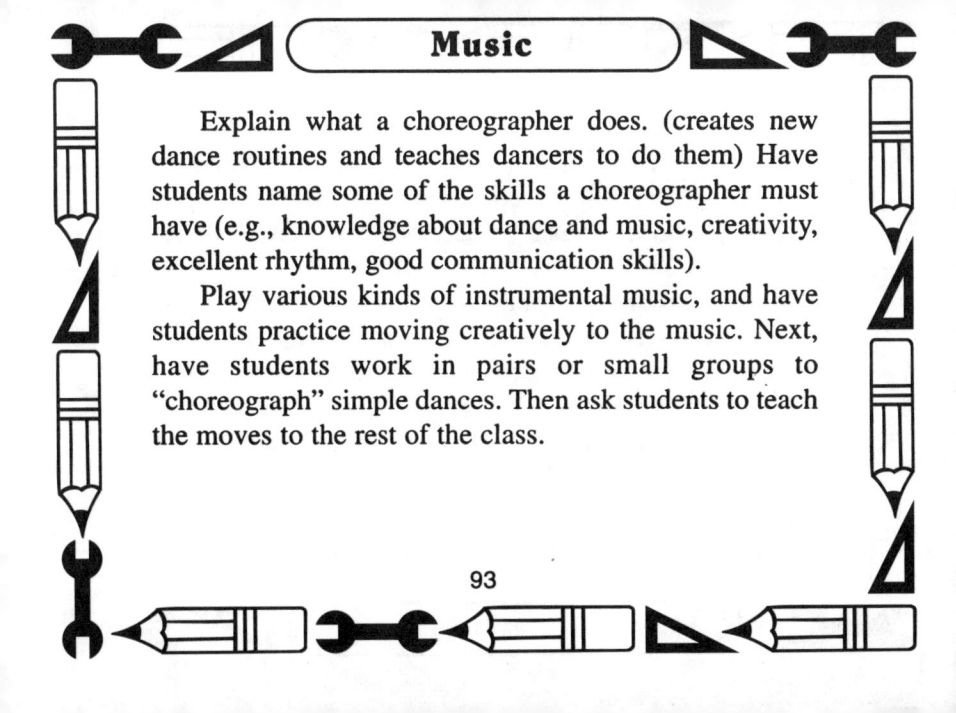

Explain what a choreographer does. (creates new dance routines and teaches dancers to do them) Have students name some of the skills a choreographer must have (e.g., knowledge about dance and music, creativity, excellent rhythm, good communication skills).

Play various kinds of instrumental music, and have students practice moving creatively to the music. Next, have students work in pairs or small groups to "choreograph" simple dances. Then ask students to teach the moves to the rest of the class.

Music

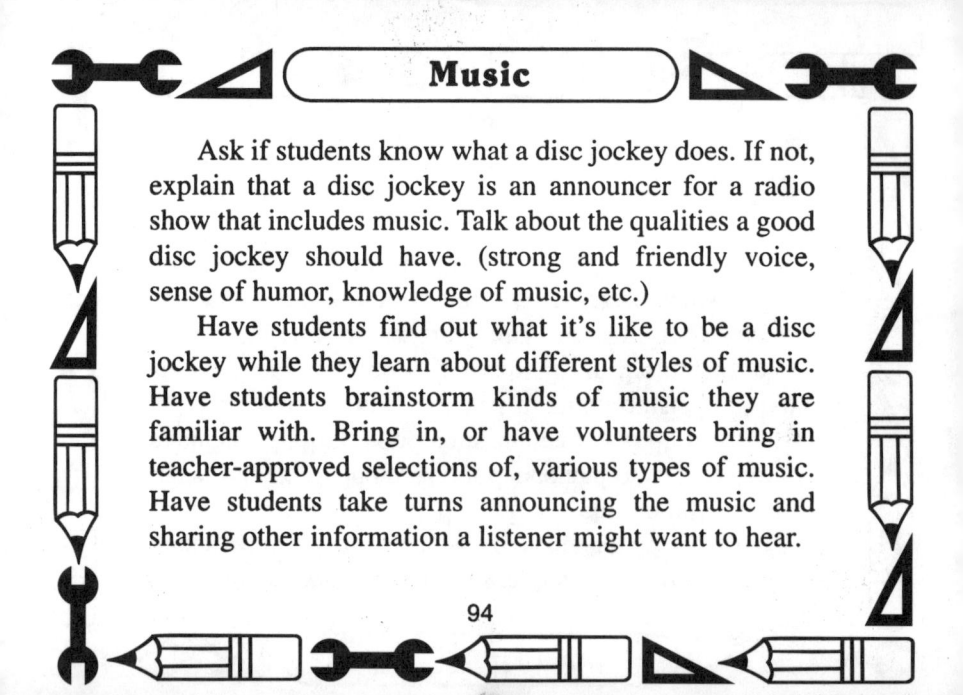

Ask if students know what a disc jockey does. If not, explain that a disc jockey is an announcer for a radio show that includes music. Talk about the qualities a good disc jockey should have. (strong and friendly voice, sense of humor, knowledge of music, etc.)

Have students find out what it's like to be a disc jockey while they learn about different styles of music. Have students brainstorm kinds of music they are familiar with. Bring in, or have volunteers bring in teacher-approved selections of, various types of music. Have students take turns announcing the music and sharing other information a listener might want to hear.